Scripture Memory Makers

Susan L. Lingo

Susan Lingo Books™

www.susanlingobooks.com

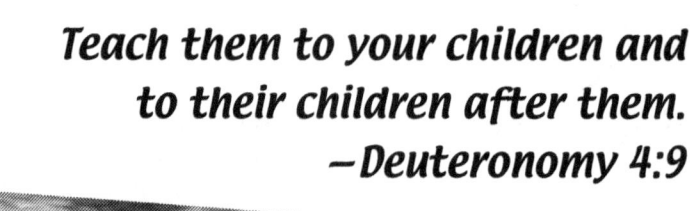

Teach them to your children and to their children after them.
—Deuteronomy 4:9

Scripture Memory Makers
© 2007 Susan L. Lingo

Published by Susan Lingo Books, Loveland, Colorado 80538. All rights reserved. No part of this book may be reproduced in any manner without written permission from the publisher, except where noted in the text and in the case of brief quotations embodied in critical articles and reviews.

Interior design and cover by Susan L. Lingo

All Scripture quotations, unless otherwise noted, are taken from the HOLY BIBLE, NEW INTERNATIONAL VERSION®, NIV®. Copyright © 1973, 1978, 1984 by International Bible Society. Used by permission of Zondervan Publishing House. All rights reserved.

16 15 14 13 12 11 10 09 08 07   5 4 3 2 1
ISBN 978-0-9760696-5-2
Printed in the United States of America

Contents

Introduction 5

Chapter One: The Gift of Memory 6

Why memory and working to learn Scripture are part of God's plan, help strengthen kids' faith for a lifetime, and demonstrate honor and and praise to God for the precious gift of His Word.

Chapter Two: The Mechanics of Memory 12

How children learn, record, and recall information through short- and long-term memory.

Chapter Three: The Fine Art of Forgetting 22

The Six Culprits of Forgetting and how to combat them; three eye-opening memory quizzes and how they demonstrate effective memory strategies for both kids and adults.

Chapter Four: Seven Super Strategies 30

The Scripture Bouquet and how each blosssom works to help children know, understand, and apply God's Word; seven powerful strategies for learning and retaining verses and passages.

Chapter Five: 3- to 6-Year-Olds 44

Interactive, age-appropriate activities, games, songs, and crafts for preschool through kindergarten-aged children; all pattern pages and reproducibles included.

Chapter Six: 7- to 12-Year-Olds 74

Interactive, age-appropriate activities, games, and crafts for children seven through twelve; all pattern pages and reproducibles included.

Basic Bible Skills Goals 102

Introduction

"All Scripture is God-Breathed and is useful for teaching, rebuking, correcting and training in righteousness, so that the man of God may be thoroughly equipped for every good work."
—2 Timothy 3:16, 17

God promises amazing things for us when we choose to honor Him by learning His Word. Our faith becomes active. We live lives that are guided and charted through God's design. We're able to embrace God's power more completely. We learn *how* to draw nearer to God and *when* to pull back from sin and temptation. We discover there are blessings and punishments—and how to live in the light of the former while learning to avoid the latter. Scripture *is* useful for equipping us to live faith-filled, obedient lives—and helping children to learn God's Word is the first step in this all-important process. Yet many teachers, pastors, and parents steer clear of encouraging their children to memorize Gods Word. After all, just knowing the gist of what God says is enough, right? *Wrong!* How can we lead kids to God's fullness if we never model learning His Word? How can we teach them obey God if we don't help them understand what God has commanded of us? And what chance do kids have of applying God's truths in their daily lives if they don't know what those truths are?

Scripture Memory Makers can help! In the pages of this powerful resource are the tools you need to help, encourage, and teach your kids—from preschool through grade school—how to learn, understand, and apply God's Word in their lives. You'll gain the essential background of what memory really is and how it works. Then you'll discover specific strategies and tools for making sure that Scripture is logged into kids' memories and hearts for a lifetime—not just on their lips for a moment! Sure, learning to remember, recall, and use God's Word takes a bit of work, but it can also be fun—and is always more than worth the time and effort. Help your kids show God their love and honor through helping them learn to know, understand, and apply His Word in their lives—you may be delightfully surprised at how many verses *you* learn, too!

Chapter One

The Gift of Memory

"The memory of the righteous will be a blessing" (Proverbs 10:7).

Among the most precious gifts God has given every man, woman, and child is the wondrous gift of memory. To the righteous, it's a blessing which offers strength, comfort, and joy. To the unrighteous, memory can be a curse of unending heart ache.

God chose to gift mankind alone with the awesome power of conscious memory. No other living, breathing organism in God's creation has the ability to memorize. Plants merely react to their physical environments. Animals learn to respond through physical reflexes, natural instincts, and conditioned responses. Salamanders can't remember sultry August days on frigid February nights. Geraniums don't recall their last sip of water. And though avid pet owners may choose to disagree, even the most faithful canines can't remember their beloved masters' names or phone numbers.

Why did God grant humans this precious gift that causes such pain and elicits such joy? To learn from! We have been given a memory that we might learn about our Father's awesome power and unfailing love. We have been granted a memory to learn about and embrace his perfect plan of Salvation through Jesus. We have been gifted with memory to learn about loving others while bearing their burdens and sharing their joys. Through memory we learn and remember what is good and evil in the eyes of our Maker and how to make Godly choices! God gave us a memory that we might learn and remember the 'holy glue' that binds all life together: Scripture.

> "God gave us a memory so that we might have roses in December."
>
> —J. M. Barrie, 1922

GOD HAS COMMANDED US TO LEARN AND MEMORIZE HIS WORD.

God has carefully and firmly set forth mighty commands concerning Scripture memorization. God said, "Fix these words of mine in your hearts and minds; tie them as symbols on your hands and bind them on your foreheads. Teach them to your children, talking about them when you sit at home and when you walk along the road, when you lie down and when you get up" (Deuteronomy 11:18). Our heavenly Father did not suggest we try to recall his words nor did he intimate we should read them once and forget them. Instead, God commanded us to impress his holy words upon our hearts, souls, hands, and minds—and upon those of our children.

In this all-important verse in Scripture, we're commanded to do four key things with God's Word:

❶ **Fix God's Words in our hearts and minds.** "Fix" in this verse comes from the Hebrew word "sin" meaning "to place or put." God desires us to place his Word in our hearts and minds; to fix and lock them deep in our inner-most parts and cradle them close to the very essence of our lives. There can be no mistaking God's intention of the word fix—God wants us to memorize his Word!

❷ **Tie God's Words to our hands.** God has commanded us to put his holy Word into action. Only when we have fixed Scripture in our hearts and minds can we apply God's Word in our lives. Even Jesus used Scripture to actively rebuke Satan's temptations.

❸ **Bind God's Words to our foreheads.** God commands us to keep Scripture foremost in our minds for when we know what God's Word says, we're able to make Godly choices in our daily walk and to readily proclaim God's truth, wisdom, and love to others.

❹ **Teach God's Word to our children.** Who can add more? God commands us to teach Scripture to our children in all we do and wherever we go! And this teaching is three-fold: memorizing, comprehending, and applying God's Word in our lives every day.

Fix. Tie. Bind. Teach. Commanding words of commitment and action—and the focus of this book. The challenging act of memorizing Scripture is obedience. It's our responsibility. And Scripture memorization can be an immense portion of our Christian joy. Jesus knew that Scripture is lifeblood which flows through our veins when he said, "Man does not live by bread alone, but on every word that comes from the mouth of God" (Matthew 4:4). If Jesus memorized and quoted Scripture, shouldn't we?

Sadly, there are some who would disagree. Their arguments range from "It's too difficult" to "Words are just words—it's action and understanding that count!" Yes, comprehension and application are vital and God-commanded, yet how can comprehension and application occur without knowing God's Word and exactly what it says? Remember "fix, tie, bind, and teach?" Fix, tie, and bind are words of **commitment** and **memory**; they precede **teaching** which is where comprehension occurs and application begins! We don't have to choose between comprehension, memorization, and application. There simply isn't a hierarchy of importance between these aspects of Scripture; they're meant to be inseparable and integral parts of one another. Isn't it wonderful that we can have the fullness of God's Word in three parts just as we have the Trinity in its three-part harmony? It's just a matter of implementing the right combination of

> *The memory of the righteous will be a blessing. —Proverbs 10:7*

Chapter One

teaching tools to help our children memorize, comprehend, and apply Scripture simultaneously!

It's impossible to understand a sentence if we lack basic phonetic skills to sound out the words. Higher mathematics mean nothing without basic number facts. So it is with God's Word. Scripture memorization is the basic foundation through which Christian comprehension and application are built. We need to know what the Word says. Then we may begin to understand its fullness and how to apply it to our lives. Read 2 Timothy 3:15: "…and how from infancy you have known the holy Scriptures, which are able to make you wise for salvation through faith in Christ Jesus."

This verse promises that through knowing Scripture we'll have wisdom—comprehension—in our Christian lives. No, our salvation doesn't rest upon our memorization prowess, but Scripture does deepen our *understanding* of the gift of salvation through Jesus!

WHY MUST WE HELP OUR CHILDREN MEMORIZE SCRIPTURE?

The act of memorization is a challenge, especially to young children who don't always understand *why* they're learning God's Word. Older children may understand more clearly, but are less driven and hard to motivate without encouragement. (How many adults are the same way?) Very small children lack basic reading and vocabulary skills to memorize Scripture. Clearly, our children need help in Scripture memorization, and it's the loving responsibility of Christian parents and teachers to carry out God's commands to lock Scripture inside His precious children.

Before moving on, let's look at the subtle difference between remembering something and memorizing it. **Remembering is the act of emotional recall.** It is being able to express the main idea or gist of a phrase or story without knowing the actual words.

Where remembrance is typically a function of emotion, memorization is a mental process whereby specific words or facts are committed to the mind and, as God has commanded us, to our hearts and souls. Memorizing is recalling much more than the gist of a sentence; it is knowing **precisely** what was said.

Though being able to recall the main idea of a story is a useful tool, it's not enough when it comes to God's Word. Ask any elementary school teacher and you'll find that young children are typically unable to choose the main idea from a story. Though children may remember story details, those details often lose something in the translation! Take for example John 14:6 when Jesus said: "I am the way and the truth and the life. No one comes to the Father except through me.'" A young child may perceive the gist of the verse as something like this: *One of the ways to God is with Jesus who's real important.* Yes, Jesus is important, but the child has missed key words in not memorizing **precisely** what was said—key words that can help us understand more clearly and powerfully who Jesus is: *the Way, the Truth, the Life—and the only pathway to God.* If our children (and ourselves as adults) are to reap the fullness of God's Word, it's imperative for us to know exactly what Scripture says!

Have you ever contemplated why God chose the words he did to include in the Bible? Exactly what is divine about Scripture? Wouldn't any words have worked as well? And if so, why did Jesus go to the trouble of memorizing God's Word and quoting Scripture? Many people spend their Christian lives trying to understand God's Word to the exclusion of memorizing even one verse! But in our human search for comprehension and logic, we're slicing off the first command God gave concerning His Word: *to fix it in our hearts and minds!* Remember, "...the wisdom in this world is foolishness in God's sight" (1 Corinthians 3:15). Let us not foolishly neglect to commit the Word of God to our memories.

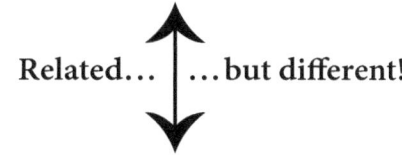

CAN MEMORY SKILLS ACTUALLY BE TAUGHT?

Yes! Memory may be strengthened in a number of ways; it's just having the right tools and strategies to help commit Scripture to mind, heart, and life. The first step is in gaining a clear understanding of how memory works and how forgetting occurs. This will help set a strong basis for memory strengthening strategies as we'll see in the next chapters.

In a world full of "quick-fixes," "instant gratification," and a "teach-me-quick" mentality, it's all too easy to toss Scripture memorization out the window. After all, it takes time and no one memorizes anything the first time they look at it. But it is possible to help our children fix Scripture inside their hearts, souls, hands, and minds. It's not the act of memorization that should be shunned, but rather the way it has (or hasn't) been taught!

WHAT MEMORIZING SCRIPTURE WILL DO FOR YOUR CHILD

"Write them (God's Word) on the door frames of your houses and on your gates, so that your days and the days of your children may be many in the

The memory of the righteous will be a blessing.—Proverbs 10:7

Chapter One

land that the LORD swore to give your forefathers, as many as the days that the heavens are above the earth" (Deuteronomy 11:20,21).

God has promised to bless and multiply his grace to both you and your child if you know his Word and live with his Word to guide your lives. Both you and your child! What a precious promise God has made us: grace from his Word!

On a more earthly level, here is what memorizing Scripture will do for your child's growing Christian walk:

- **STRENGTHENING POWER!** Having a ready command of Scripture will help your child overcome worry, fear, self doubt, and loneliness. Your child will live confidently in God's perfect peace, knowing God's promises, and having them written in his heart to recall in times of distress and discouragement.

➤ **Your word is a lamp to my feet and a light for my path** (Psalm 119:105).

➤ He sent forth his word and healed them (Psalm 107:20).

- **HELP IN OVERCOMING SIN!** Even Jesus quoted Scripture when Satan tempted him in the wilderness. Three times Jesus rebuked Satan with the words: "For it is written…" before quoting the only weapon effective against Satan—the Word of God! Once impressed upon heart and soul, God's Word becomes the powerful "sword of the spirit"—there when your child is waging battles of right and wrong and helping him or her make Godly decisions.

➤ **I have hidden your word in my heart that I might not sin against you.** (Psalm 119:11)

➤ **Take the helmet of salvation and the sword of the Spirit, which is the word of God.** (Ephesians 6:17)

- **POWER IN WITNESSING!** Knowing God's Word and being able to confidently proclaim it, will enable your child to shout aloud the wonderful message of salvation through Jesus Christ. Being able to recite Scripture will help your child tell others about God's faithfulness—from peers at school to the shopkeeper down the street, your little one will become God's messenger of love and truth!

➤ He must hold firmly to the trustworthy message as it has been taught, so that he can encourage others by sound doctrine and refute those who oppose it. (Titus 1:9)

➤ Preach the Word; be prepared in season and out of season; correct, rebuke and encourage. (2 Timothy 4:2)

- **DRAWING NEARER THE LORD!** God's Word infuses God's love and truth into your child's life! Reading, learning, and committing Scripture to heart, soul, hands, and mind will lead to deeper faith and stronger reliance as your child sees how God keeps his Word and perfect faithfulness.

► **Come near to God and he will come near to you.** (James 4:8a)

► **How sweet are your words to my taste, sweeter than honey to my mouth!** (Psalm 119:103)

The time you share in joyously helping your child lock God's precious Word in his or her heart (and your own!) will become some of the sweetest times you'll ever share with your child. Quiet time spent in God's Word can be compared to few other moments—and sharing this time with your child is truly a God-given gift!

You're about to begin helping your child toward a lifetime of gathering the most precious of childhood collections. Among his rock collections, stamps, buttons, butterflies, and sea shell collections, none will be more cherished or life sustaining than your child's Scripture collection! Gathered in heart, displayed in his life, your child's Scripture collection will continually grow in depth, size, and value throughout his entire lifetime. Rejoice in the sharing; revel in the love. You are doing God's will for your child!

The time you share joyously helping your child learn God's Word will be some of the sweetest times you'll ever share—and having a command of Scripture will help your child overcome worry, fear, self-doubt, and loneliness later in life.

The memory of the righteous will be a blessing. —Proverbs 10:7

Chapter Two

Mechanics of Memory

From the moment of birth, we're bombarded by countless sensory experiences, physical stimuli, and verbal and non-verbal communications. All learning is channeled through these experiences and in these ways we learn to react to and upon our surroundings. Memory plays a crucial role in our ability to remember responses we may choose to repeat or avoid.

Consider for a moment all your child has been learning physically, emotionally, spiritually, and socially. Your child has learned various methods of communication which include gestures, words, and facial expressions. He or she has learned and perhaps mastered physical skills such as walking, running, skipping, and riding two wheel bicycles. If your child is in school, he or she is involved in learning number concepts, phonetics, and how to express him or herself on paper. The number of concepts your child is learning are endless!

Of course all this learning would be useless if God had not gifted your child with remembrance and memory. Without memory, your child would respond to each situation as if it were new and would not gather lessons to put to use later in life. Without memory, there would be no learning. Without memory, your child's reasoning, discernment, and self perceptions would be non-existent. And without memory, your child would even forget the Lord, his love, and his plan of salvation! Thank you, Father, for the precious gift of memory!

> **And even if only one good memory is left in our hearts, it may also be the instrument of our salvation one day.**
>
> —Foedor Dostoyevsky

Your child is learning at break-neck speed, but learning doesn't stop with the advent of adolescence or adulthood. The lessons we've stored in our memories serve as foundations for continual learning through our final earthly breath. Though most basic skills are learned and mastered by the time a child reaches the eighth grade, higher learning and reasoning yield the fruits of creativity, invention, and application. If it weren't for memory, there would be no medical breakthroughs, no sophisticated communication systems, no poetry or art. Memory can be thought of as the foundation of learning, but to make that foundation functional and solid, we must understand how memory works. The more we understand about the process of memorization, the better equipped we'll become to help our children effectively memorize the Word of God.

THREE WAYS CHILDREN STORE LEARNING

It's Tuesday afternoon in Mrs. Wigby's music class. Dane, Emily, and Lindsay are clutching the instruments their parents bought in hopes of their playing one day in the high school's marching band. Mrs. Wigby enters the room and sweeps past Emily, bumping her elbow against the girl rather callously. She shoots a pleasant smile toward Dane and says, "Greetings, young man. So glad you're here!" Dane smiles and replies, "Good morning." Then Mrs.. Wigby helps Lindsay begin practicing the musical scales they've worked on for four weeks.

Later, the three students recall their Tuesday afternoon music class with Mrs. Wigby. Emily didn't enjoy music class or Mrs. Wigby—she felt as if she was invisible. Dane, on the other hand, thought Mrs. Wigby was quite friendly and he's looking forward to next week's music lesson. Lindsay was confident she knew the music scales and felt as though her fingers flew over the instrument; she barely even noticed Mrs. Wigby.

How could all three children have responded so radically different to the same teacher and music class? What perceptions stayed in their memories and why? We respond to learning and store that information in three distinct ways; through: developed skills, verbal responses, and emotional responses. As we briefly examine each of these concepts, try to identify the particular ways Emily, Dane, and Lindsay responded to Mrs. Wigby and her music class.

SKILLS. Your child may have already set aside the training wheels and is off and pedaling a new two wheeled bicycle, proud and pleased of this newfound freedom. Learning how to ride a bicycle is a learned skill. Skills involve the use of the physical body and are the most basic of learning. Once mastered, a skill is recalled as reflex, requiring little use of conscious memory. What is that old saying? *Once you learn to ride a bike you never forget!* The body may be older and less agile but the know-how never leaves. And so it is with swimming, jogging, painting, or bowling. You may have to polish a skill to give it your own personal touch or shine up rusty age spots, but the basic skill is retained with little need of digging into conscious memory.

VERBAL RESPONSES. As your child began hearing you refer to that glass of white stuff as "milk," he or she began to form a relationship between that good tasting white stuff and the verbal word "milk." Soon your child began to imitate that verbal sound whenever he or she referred to milk. It's doubtful that your child now has to dig into his or her memory in search of that particular word.

Our children learn approximately 2,500 different words before the age of five and are not only able to repeat these words, they have an understanding of what most represent. From constant reiteration, verbal responses are locked into memory and soon, without much thought, young children are able to respond to questions, express feelings and ideas, and communicate with no real thought to pulling from their memory stores of vocabulary. Speaking becomes spontaneous.

Your word is a lamp to my feet and a light for my path. —Psalm 119:105

Chapter Two

EMOTIONAL RESPONSES. The third way of responding to learning deals with emotion. This is perhaps the most crucial learning stage as it does not deal with physical or verbal reflex, but with emotions and gut level feelings. Though memory born of emotional response is not reflexive in nature, it's what ultimately locks learning inside a child's (or adult's) heart. Because you screamed when that innocent garden snake slithered over your toes, your child may also have learned to be frightened of snakes. This is an emotional response and will not easily be forgotten!

Emotional responses are extremely powerful for they involve our innermost feelings and little common sense or logic. Emotional responses are 'gut reactions' and if the emotional response that is triggered is extremely negative or positive, it won't easily be forgotten with the passage of time. It's as difficult to forget that first kiss as it is to erase the personal encounter with a snake!

> **EMOTIONAL RESPONSES** remain in your memory the longest.
>
> **SKILLS** remain next longest.
>
> **VERBAL RESPONSES** are most readily forgotten.

Of the three main ways people log learning into memory, psychologists believe that emotional responses remain inside the memory the longest followed by skills and verbal responses. This information is vital in our quest to help children memorize Scripture. Merely repeating the words of a verse sets the stage for memory-loss, but helping children *emote* the feelings behind the verse not only aids comprehension, it increases the chances of binding Scripture into hearts and minds.

What about Emily, Lindsay, and Dane? Emily reacted to Mrs. Wigby with an *emotional response.* Because of the negative physical contact and no response from Mrs. Wigby, Emily perceived her music teacher as cold and insensitive—Emily learned that music class was "yucky." Dane's positive reaction to Mrs. Wigby was a *verbal response.* Mrs. Wigby spoke pleasantly to Dane, thus he perceived her as friendly and responsive. Dane learned that his teacher and music class are enjoyable. Lindsay's response was *skill oriented.* She stored learning through physically playing her instrument and though she barely noticed her teacher, Lindsay confidently learned to play music.

WHAT ARE THE THREE R's OF MEMORY?

Remember grade school and the three R's of those long ago school days? Reading, 'riting, and 'rithmetic were the quintessential view of effective learning. The study of memory also has 3 R's: Recording, retaining, and recalling (or retrieval), and it's within these three progressive stages that materials enter the memory. When material is learned, it travels through each of these stages in order. Each stage is a vital link in permanent memory and teaching must occur through all three crucial stages. Let's briefly explore the 3 R's of memory and how each works in relation to the other.

RECORDING — Recording is the initial stage of memory and it's here that whatever is to be memorized is first introduced. This is the easiest stage of memory to teach, but also the stage where 90% of learned material is lost before it travels to stage two! This is often where many Scripture memory clubs and classroom memory work fail—they never teach beyond the point of recording a verse. It's no wonder critics of Scripture memorization point contentious fingers and say memorization is useless! But the simple fact is, *these children never memorized Scripture in the first place—they merely repeated sentences.* Teaching and repetition must continue through the next two stages before actual memorization occurs.

RETAINING — Stage two in the process of memorization is *retention* where what has been learned is kept until it's needed. Retention is often lost through neglecting to practice or apply what's been learned; without reinforcement, retention is minimal. As in the case of recording, simply asking a child to repeat a verse moments after hearing it does not constitute solid learning of that verse. To combat retention-detention, work on one Scripture verse at a time and be sure it's thoroughly learned before tackling a new verse. Remember, similarity of activity inhibits memorization. It's important not to overwhelm your child with learning more than one verse of Scripture at a time.

RECALLING — Recall or *retrieval* is the final stage of committing learned material to memory and it's by far the most difficult stage. Recall is in essence, locating stored material and bringing it out to be used or repeated. There are a great number of *memory triggers* and tricks to aid your child's recall. The majority of this book is devoted to tooling you through the stage of recall and providing you with effective strategies for enabling children to carry God's Word on their lips as well as in their hearts and lives!

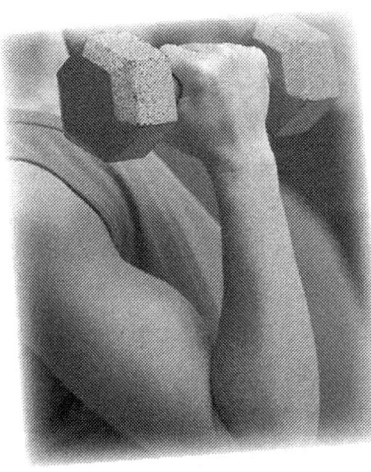

Remember: recording, retaining, and recall are all crucial steps in the memorization process and each occurs in sequential order. If any stage is missing or weak, permanent memory is nearly impossible!

Just as repetitions with weights build muscle, practicing and repeating Scripture builds memory muscle!

Your word is a lamp to my feet and a light for my path. —Psalm 119:105

Chapter Two

SHORT AND LONG-TERM MEMORY

Learned material falls into two memory categories: *short-term memory* and *long-term memory*. Everything we experience is eventually logged into one of these two storage systems. It's important to understand how each works before applying logical strategies to help children memorize Scripture.

SHORT-TERM MEMORY

Short-term memory refers to how many items may be remembered correctly at one time or how much a person may consciously pay attention to simultaneously. Short-term memory is closely related to attention span. Just as short attention spans make learning challenging, short-term memory challenges the amount of learning that takes place. Here's why.

Short-term memory has a rapid rate of forgetting. If what has been learned is not continually repeated it will be forgotten. In other words, "if you don't use it, you lose it!" Most incoming information is forgotten within 30 seconds. In fact, people who aren't expecting a memory test can seldom remember three consonants out of ten after only two seconds of distraction. *Two seconds.* Finally! Parents and teachers have proof that some things we say and teach actually do go in one ear and out the other.

The rapid rate of forgetting in short-term memory may be illustrated by an experience more familiar than many of us care to admit. How often have you looked up a telephone number only to forget it by the time you reach the phone? It's only after you look it up again that you'll remember the number. Take heart! You're not getting older and more forgetful—you're just a victim of your own short-term memory!

In addition to a rapid rate of forgetting, short-term memory has an extremely limited capacity. For most people that capacity is only seven sequential items whether they're numbers, shapes, or words. Try this little experiment with a friend. Repeat a list of four numbers, then have your partner repeat them in order. Add one new numeral per second and have your friend quickly repeat them in correct order each time a new number is added. By the time you reach seven or eight numbers, your partner probably won't remember them long enough to repeat them accurately on the first try.

A Closer Look

Combat the high rate of forgetting through *repetition*. Repeating a Scripture verse over a period of time allows the verse to soak into your child's memory.

> Did you know that most new information is usually forgotten within 30 seconds?

Offer smaller portions of Scripture to younger children. Bite-sized pieces are always easier to chew and swallow!

Using seven words as a wonderful guide, try offering children shorter, easier verses—or even partial verses for very young children. Isaiah 53:6a is a good example: "We all, like sheep, have gone astray." Your child will be able to handle this portion of Scripture as it contains only seven words. Help your child master this portion of the verse while explaining the second half, then in time you may add the next portion of the verse quite easily.

Short-term memory has a high rate of forgetting and is very limited in the amount of what may be stored. Of what practical use, then, is short-term memory? Because of its rapid forgetting rate, short-term memory helps us 'weed out' stimuli which is not important enough to store for any length of time. Of all the bits of daily trivia we hear, learn, and see, few actually need to be retained for future use. If we recalled everything we had ever experienced from birth we'd certainly explode from overload! Short-term memory also helps us stay focused on an immediate goal or learning activity. Without short-term memory to help us recall from minute to minute, we'd whip from one activity to the next and never allow learning to sink in.

Both of these pluses make short-term memory an important step in helping our children memorize Scripture. But short-term memory won't permanently fix God's Word in children's hearts or minds. For this we must turn to long-term memory.

The Good & Bad of Short-Term Memory

Weak Points	Strong Points
Information is quickly forgotten	Weeds out information not needed.
Amount of information is very limited.	Helps us stay focused.

LONG TERM MEMORY

Long-term memory is what most people refer to when they speak of memory. Simply stated, long-term memory is stored learning that remains in your conscious and unconscious mind. It's memory that lasts a lifetime; however—and here's the catch—not everything stored in long-term memory is easy to recall.

Return for a moment to that filing cabinet. You may think of long-term memory as the filing cabinet itself with easy to recall memories kept in the top drawer, often recalled memories in the middle drawer, and buried memories stuffed and hidden in the bottom drawer. The bottom drawer holds memories that are long ago and far away or memories that may be too painful for the conscious mind to recall easily.

Your word is a lamp to my feet and a light for my path.—Psalm 119:105

Chapter Two

Storing learned Scripture verses in the long-term memory files of children is the goal. The real challenge is in storing those verses in the *top drawer* to be easily and readily recalled throughout their entire lives. So the logical question becomes: How can we help children commit Scripture to long-term memory? First you must be aware of the three triggers that channel learning into long-term memory:

❶ KNOWING THE WHY

❷ RECITING THE WHAT

❸ FEELING THE WHO

KNOWING THE WHY. Realizing how or why something works as it does gives a child a clearer understanding of the object or concept and makes memorization *relevant*. Comprehension is an important component in memorization and may be used effectively in Scripture memory by discussing the meaning behind each verse you're working on. God wants children to fully understand His truth—not just the sounds of the words. When children begin to understand the "why" of Scripture, they begin putting the verse into action as it's memorized into heart and mind. This is important for those who feel that Scripture comprehension should be stressed over memorization. Clearly, one can't occur without the other if we're to gain God's Word in it's fullness.

RECITING THE WHAT. Only when learned material is reinforced continually over time can it be committed to long-term memory. Short-term memory allows for recitation within minutes or even hours, but only long-term memory allows verses to be repeated days, weeks, and even months after being learned. If a verse is reviewed and recited at periodic times, children should be able to recite a Scripture verse years after they have learned it!

Just as songs create powerful feelings, so can Scripture. Use the connection with kids to last a lifetime!

FEELING THE WHO. If you'll remember back to the three ways we respond to learning (through skills, verbal responses, and emotional responses), you'll see a striking similarity between learned emotional responses and personal feelings in long-term memory. Whenever we experience emotion in conjunction with learning, the learned material becomes easy to recall even after many years. Hearing a particular melody at the supermarket may transport you back to your first day of school when the kindergarten teacher played the same melody as you sat missing your mother. Years later, your jaw tightens as you remember the song and the ache of being away from momma for the first time. Personal feelings are powerful memory makers!

WHAT'S THE CONNECTION BETWEEN SHORT AND LONG-TERM MEMORY?

Let's return to the filing cabinet concept to help clarify the relationship between short-term and long-term memory, only now we'll add an "IN" basket. The IN basket will represent short-term memory, and the large filing cabinet long-term memory. When learned materials arrive at the office, they're put into the IN basket. The IN basket has very limited capacity and can only hold so much before it must be emptied to make room for more materials.

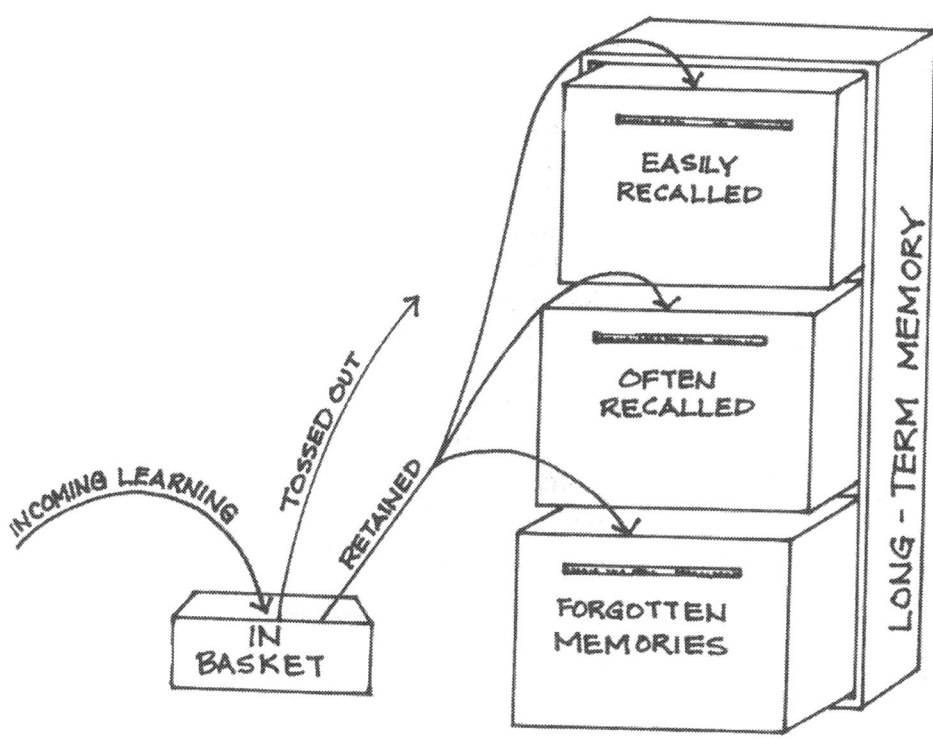

When the IN basket is sorted, some material is tossed out for lack of need. Some material is used immediately, then discarded. And other materials are filed away in the large filing cabinet of long-term memory. Nothing is put into the filing cabinet that has not been first routed through the IN basket.

In the same way, everything your child hears, sees, learns, and experiences goes into the short-term IN basket. But because the IN basket's capacity is so limited, much material is thrown out before it's filed in the long-term filing cabinet. The key to transferring Scripture verses from short-term to long-term memory is in finding effective, age appropriate ways to store these verses for lifetime recollection.

Your word is a lamp to my feet and a light for my path. —Psalm 119:105

Chapter Two

A Closer Look

Many teachers and parents question the validity of memorizing Scripture—that most kids only need to know the gist of God's Word and can't remember verses anyway. But if a child has trouble recalling a verse, it's probably because the verse wasn't really memorized at all! Remember: A verse needs to reach the stage of long-term memory before it is truly memorized—and this takes time, perseverance, and patience!

Perhaps you're having a bit of trouble remembering all that has been discussed in this chapter! Not to worry; there won't be any memory tests—yet! But a brief summary of all we have covered will help reinforce what you've learned. Remember, repetition is key for retention!

The 3 R's of memory:

- ***Recording*** (initial learning)
- ***Retaining*** (keeping learned material until it's needed)
- ***Recalling*** (retrieving what's been learned)

Two storage systems for memory:

- ***Short-term memory*** (through which all learned material passes)
- ***Long-term memory*** (knowing the why, reciting the what, and feeling the who)

A little review helps, doesn't it? It would boggle our minds if we knew the number of review hours it must have taken Hebrew children in biblical days to memorize the entire Torah—the first five books of the Bible. Because God had commanded them to learn His Word and because little was written down so long ago, the Hebrews relied upon strong, long-term memories to quote the Word of God. Even children were expected to carry on God's Word through oral recitation. It hardly seems possible and yet it *was* possible!

You have a clearer understanding of how memory works and this will be of great help in formulating effective learning strategies for helping your children with Scripture memorization. But this is only half the coin. We'll complete our study with a brief journey into the realm of … forgetting. For only when we know how to battle forgetting, will we remember how to memorize!

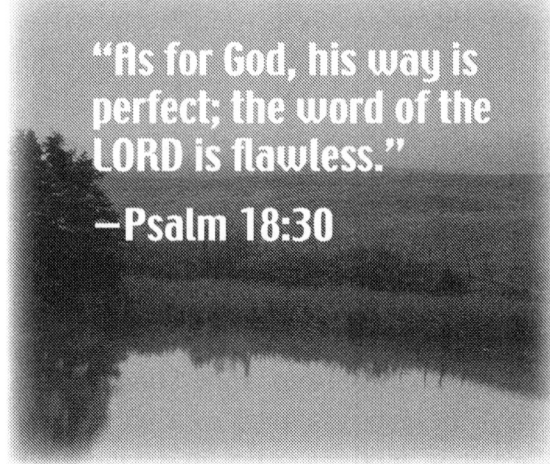

"As for God, his way is perfect; the word of the LORD is flawless."
—Psalm 18:30

Your word is a lamp to my feet and a light for my path. —Psalm 119:105

Chapter Three

The Fine Art of Forgetting

"The effectiveness of our memory banks is determined not by the total number of facts we take in, but the number we wish to reject."
—Jon Wynne-Tyson, 1975

In our discussion of short-term memory, we learned that a portion of what we forget is not all bad. If we didn't have the capacity to forget, our minds would be jumbled with countless details and tiny incidentals that would make it impossible to find, select, and use information we need for decision making. A certain amount of forgetting is necessary—the trick is to forget the trivial while retaining the important!

You know from experience that forgetting things is much easier than remembering them, but why? A clue lies in the 3 R's of memory—the stages of Recording, Retaining, and Recalling. To forget something, you need only fail at one of these stages. But to *remember* important information, all three stages must be in solid working order. In other words, there's one chance to remember and three chances to forget! Those aren't comforting odds for most of us.

50% of what has just been learned will be forgotten in the next hour!

By now you have a clearer understanding of memory and how it works. Now let's turn our attention to the mechanics of forgetting so you can combat it in helping children (and yourself) memorize God's Word.

WHY WE FORGET

Read the following series of grocery items:

milk, potatoes, butter, cheese, ice cream, cabbage, eggs, meat, soap, bananas

With a little practice, your child could remember these ten items. But without repeating them often, the items on the list would be immediately forgotten. How quickly do we forget? The greatest memory loss occurs within the first 60 minutes of learning. In the case of the grocery list above, only five items may be remembered after one hour. A day or two later, your child might recall one or two of the items. Within a week it's almost certain your child would remember none of them. *Time* is an important factor in why we forget information. As time goes on a person forgets more and more of what has been learned. Like an ocean swallowing a wave, time may eventually swallow learning.

Time isn't the only factor affecting why we forget. *Lack of repetition* is another contributor. When what has been learned is not repeated, reviewed, reread, or reinforced periodically over time, it will be forgotten. Through periodic review and reinforcement of what's been learned, memory retention is greatly strengthened. The key to repetition is in making it motivating and on-going. Merely reviewing a lesson or Scripture verse once or twice won't cut it—reinforcement must continue through all three stages of memory.

Six Culprits of Forgetting

- Time
- Lack of repetition
- When learned
- Similarity of activity
- Age
- Diet
- Attitude

Think back to the time your child was learning the Alphabet song. Unless your child is a genius or has a photographic memory, you probably sang the song so many times you were singing it in your sleep. It was through repetition of the song over a period of time that fixed the alphabet in your child's memory. And now your child can sing the song in his or her sleep! The same principle applies when helping children memorize Scripture. Repetition over time will allow God's Word to become fixed in memory—and what a beautiful song to remember!

The third component of forgetting revolves around **when an item is learned**. Fascinating studies have proven that a person will remember more accurately and clearly any learning that takes place just before bedtime. Why is this? Events over the course of a day may interfere greatly with learning so by day's end, what was learned in the morning may be the farthest thing from mind.

Learning becomes buried under all that transpires during the day, especially for children who are not as focused as adults. Hours of school, different subjects, friends, television, family, and a host of other busy activities and distractions fill a child's day. Couple this with a shortened attention span and it's no wonder our little ones have a difficult time recalling Scripture verses learned in church once a week.

When daytime learning is combined with bedtime review, memory is greatly strengthened. This is a clear indication that evening Scripture time may be most effective, and surely a more pleasant and relaxed time for sharing. Make the most of quiet, evening Scripture times. Bedtime review and a quick

I will never forget your precepts . . . —Psalm 119:93

Chapter Three

reinforcement time over breakfast and dinner will begin and end your child's day with God's Word and is a wonderful habit to begin nurturing now!

In addition to time, lack of repetition, and when something is learned, *similarity of activity* is key in the precarious balance of something remembered and something forgotten. When you try to do two things at once, one is bound to suffer. Learning to ride a bike has little effect on memorizing John 3:16. They're dissimilar activities. But trying to memorize both John 3:16 and Isaiah 53:6 simultaneously can be extremely difficult as both are similar activities, involving the memorization of words, phrases, and numbers.

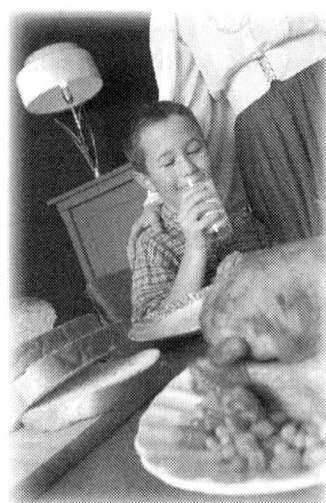

Mealtimes offer good times to discuss and review memory verses.

Make certain your child has attained a level of mastery of one verse before moving on to a new one, but continue reviewing the learned verse regularly. Once a verse has been satisfactorily learned, you may use more than one verse at a time for review sessions.

There are a few additional factors that may affect memory in children. Educators are very aware of these factors that parents often overlook.

AGE

Children may be taught nearly any Scripture verse provided it is taught or presented in an *age appropriate* way. Three-year-olds are not too young for Scripture memory work if you choose a verse that is short and contains easy words. Use a Bible written specifically for children as translations are simpler and presented in more child-like terms. "Jesus wept" (John 11:35) is a powerful verse for the tiniest of beginning Scripture scholars and leads to a lovely illustration of how even Jesus felt great sadness and cried. Allow your little ones to feel the meaning of verses to help lock their meaning inside.

DIET

Well-nourished bodies help maintain well-nourished brains. Studies have repeatedly shown that in underdeveloped countries where nutrition is poor or non-existent, children's ability to concentrate is greatly impaired—and concentration is critical for memory! Broccoli, spinach, and other leafy green vegetables are nourishing brain food—but they're probably not your child's favorite choices. Calling these special brain foods "Scripture food" may delight your child and encourage first (or even second) helpings.

ATTITUDE

A motivated attitude works wonders with memory! Positive attitudes not only make learning Scripture easier, they foster a feeling of joy at accomplishment. Unfortunately, our children aren't always intrinsically motivated. But take heart—there are ways to nurture motivation and positive, cooperative attitudes. One way is to incorporate fun, snappy games and activities designed for children in age appropriate ways. Not only will fun activities motivate children, they will effectively strengthen Scripture memory simultaneously. Through stimulating, hands-on games and activities, children learn to "do." And when we offer children lively, concrete activities, they learn more effectively and retain learning longer. Nurturing a positive attitude toward memorizing God's Word is a wonderful gift to give your child!

After 30 days, students remember:

10% of what they HEAR.

20% of what they SEE.

40% of what they DISCUSS.

80% of what they DO!

Time, age, lack of repetition, and the other fiends of forgetting *can* be overcome and the way paved to effective learning and memorization. Remember: **You can count on God's help as you and your children memorize His Word.**

And now for a little fun!

We've taken a close look at memory and how it works. We've discussed the fine art of forgetting and how quickly we master it. You may be wondering just how good your own memory skills are and how specific techniques can be used to strengthen it. Before we move on to helping children with verses, let's have a little interactive, educational fun with your own memory!

In the following pages are three Memory Quotient (MQ) quizzes. Each quiz is simple and will contain hints and strategies to help you improve your score. These pages will begin to tool you with practical, effective strategies to put to immediate use in helping your children memorize Scripture. Chapter 4 will build and expand upon many of these engaging and effective strategies. Remember, these quizzes are simply for fun *and* learning!

I will never forget your precepts…
—Psalm 119:93

Chapter Three

MQ QUIZ 1

• • • • • • • • • • • • • •

Stare at the following list for 10 seconds, then immediately cover the list and write it sequentially on the blank spaces.

___ ___ ___ ___ ___ ___ ___ ___

Now count the number of items you listed correctly.
- 0-2 correct .... Average
- 3-4 correct .... Great
- 5-6 correct .... Amazing
- 7 correct   .... Pray your kids inherit your MQ!

Well, how did you fare? If you're like most people, you scored only two or three items in their correct order. Want a rematch? Stare at the list of shapes for another 10 seconds, then cover them up and draw them below.

___ ___ ___ ___ ___ ___ ___ ___

Did you check your score? Much better! Why did you improve the second time? There were three memory strengthening strategies at work:

- **Repetition.** You repeated the test twice and this helped fix the shapes in your mind. Chances are you were even able to "see" the shapes in your mind's eye. Repeating material places it in short-term memory, but if you aren't working to recall information over the next few hours or days, it will soon be forgotten.

- **Familiar comprehension.** Before you took this test, it was unfamiliar to you. You had no idea how many shapes you'd see or why you needed to recall their order. The second time you took the test, it was no longer unfamiliar—you understood what you were to do, how many shapes you had to recall, and you were on the lookout for their sequential order.

- **Recording.** People often overlook an extremely important aspect of learning—*recording* what's to be learned using words or drawings. When something is committed to paper, it increases the chance of being recorded in the mind. Physically drawing the shapes helped fix them mentally in your brain. There's a powerful correlation between physically recording information and mentally remembering it!

MQ QUIZ 2

Read the following list. Then cover it up and write the items on the blanks. Don't worry about the order, simply see if you're able to recall all eight items.

1. lettuce   _____
2. apples   _____
3. pudding   _____
4. tissue paper   _____
5. corn on the cob   _____
6. napkins   _____
7. bananas   _____
8. detergent   _____

Now count the number of items you listed correctly.
- 0-3 .... **Average**
- 4-7 .... **Super**
- 8 .... **Please do my shopping this week!**

This time, create your *own* list using the same items. Alphabetize the items, group them according to categories, or whatever you devise. Then cover the list and write it again in the second column.

_____   _____
_____   _____
_____   _____
_____   _____
_____   _____
_____   _____
_____   _____
_____   _____

Was your score better this time? It should have been; you used two powerful memory strategies the second time around!

- **Personalizing.** When you created your own method of listing the items, you made this cold, insensitive grocery list personal—you gave the list a portion of yourself. Personalizing the material is a great way to fix it in your mind.

- **Lumping or alphabetizing.** Chances are you either grouped items into categories or alphabetized them. Putting items into similar groups or using a common tool such as the alphabet helps order items for easy recall.

You've already used five great strategies for strengthening your memory. See if you can put any of them to use in the next Memory Quotient quiz!

I will never forget your precepts . . .
—Psalm 119:93

MQ QUIZ 3

Look at the rows of shapes below for 15 seconds. Then cover them up and draw both rows in order.

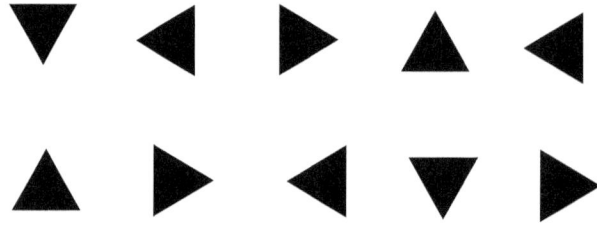

▼ ◄ ► ▲ ◄

▲ ► ◄ ▼ ►

— — — — —

— — — — —

Whew! Perhaps it's best if we don't score this tough test at all! This is a difficult test, but not unlike asking your child to memorize two Scripture verses at once or to begin learning a new verse when the former wasn't well learned. This is an illustration of *similar activity*—of attempting to memorize two lists that are closely related. Whether it's shapes or similar words, this is hard to do!

Scripture verses often contain nearly identical words and phrases. And since all verses have reference numbers, it makes them even more challenging to memorize. Stop and think of all the chapter 1, verse 5's there are in the Bible—all 66 of them! Confusing for children, yes, but there are ways to effectively memorize similar verses and references. As for this test? Try the following technique…

➡ Go back to the shapes in MQ 3 and look at them one by one, going across the page. Any patterns to the points of the triangles? Yes! Down, up, left, right, down, up. Now compare each triangle, top to bottom in pairs. Any patterns? Well, what do you know. The bottom row of triangles is exactly opposite from the top!

Look for patterns in verses—you'll be surprised how this strategy helps kids remember similar verses better!

Looking for *patterns* in similar verses help your child organize the words. Patterns may include rhyming words, words that begin with similar letter sounds, opposites, rhythmic words and phrases, syllable counts, and more. Help your children notice any similarity in how each verse begins or what each verse is saying.

• • • • • • • • • • • • • • • • • •

With an idea of how your own memory is shaping up and a few new tools to strengthen it, we're ready to move on to specific strategies which will help your child better recall God's Word.

Remind older children that, like memorizing musical notes on an instrument, learning God's Word takes time and technique, too!

Try This!

Older kids love taking the simple Memeory Quotient tests you just took—and the quizzes help kids better understand the challenges of memorizing along with the effectiveness of certain memory strategies!

I will never forget your precepts . . .
—Psalm 119:93

Chapter Four

Seven Super Strategies for Memorizing

• • • • • • • • • •

"It wasn't easy memorizing Scripture as a kid, but it's the only thing that's carried me through some very rough times as an adult." —Barbara, age 46

Who said memorizing God's Word is easy? God didn't tell us it would be without challenge, but few worthwhile things in life are. Many people claim they can't memorize, yet they can and do memorize many of the most "trivial" things: Aunt LuLu's birthday, drivers' license numbers, favorite chili recipes, even grocery lists. Why? These are things that probably won't help us through hard times, offer comfort or reassurance, or deepen our understanding of life. Yet many people spend more time memorizing trivial fluff than working even ten minutes a year memorizing the God's Word!

God didn't promise that learning, understanding, or applying His Word would be easy—but He did promise His Word would be truthful, helpful, sustaining, and powerful! God will open doors to those who take the effort and time to learn His Word and has equipped us with marvelous tools to strengthen our memory muscle. It's up to us to step through the door and apply these tools!

Identifying the Scripture Bouquet

Certain basic principles of learning set the foundation for effective Scripture memory in children. These principles are easily applied to memorizing any verse in the Bible—and memorizing nearly anything outside of Scripture as well. David, through God's inspiration, equipped us with three powerful steps toward memorization through the following praise phrases from Psalms:

> "With my lips I recount all the laws that come from your mouth. I rejoice in following your statutes as one rejoices in great riches. I meditate on your precepts and consider your ways. I delight in your decrees; I will not neglect your word." (Psalm 119:13-16)

Consider the following phrases: "With my lips I recount…" "I meditate on your precepts…" "I will not neglect your word." These three phrases hold God's steps for committing Scripture to children's minds, hearts, and lips for a lifetime. The best way of examining these powerful steps is through the *Scripture Bouquet*. Let's explore this 3-step teaching process that will help Scripture "blossom" in your children!

The Scripture Bouquet helps kids and adults remember the three steps to memorizing God's Word.

Step 1: TULIPS (oral recitation)

"With my lips I will recount…" (Psalm 119:13a) David's 119th Psalm is a passionate, inspired love poem to God's Word. David realized that Scripture is more than a collection of lifeless words—it's life-sustaining and the only constant in a world filled with pain, uncertainty, and temptation. David realized that merely reading or knowing the gist of the Word wasn't enough; he strove to have God's Word on his lips and in his heart.

The first step in fixing God's Word in your child's memory is in orally reciting the verse with his or her two lips—hence the step of tu-lips. Upon initial presentation of a particular verse, encourage your child to verbally repeat the verse at least five times and until the entire verse is recited completely and correctly. As a rule, this is accomplished in one sitting.

Oral repetition allows your child to become familiar with the sounds of the words, the order of the words, and to begin realizing what the verse is saying. Recitation also facilitates recall. In essence, when you recite you're actually rehearsing retrieval. Though verbal recitation is the first step in memorizing God's Word, it won't lock a particular verse in long-term memory by itself. The Tulip Step is a short-term memory skill and it's imperative to teach through the next step: *The Roses.*

A Closer Look

In a fascinating study of memory and recall by J. F. King, E. B. Zechmeister, and J. J. Shaughnessy, a group of students listened to five lists, each containing ten items. The lists were repeated three times. Half of the students *recited* each list after it was read while the other group simply *listened* to the lists. There was no notable difference in memory or recall between the two groups after 10-minutes, but 48-hours later the recitation group performed significantly better in recalling the items on each list. Recitation makes an impressive difference!

I have hidden your word in my heart….
—Psalm 119:11

Chapter Four

STEP 2: ROSES (understanding the verse)

"I meditate on your precepts ... and consider your ways," (Psalm 119:15) We saw earlier how strong emotions aid memory recall as in the case of a first kiss—or receiving a beautiful rose from someone special. Applying that same principle, we need to create in our children strong, emotional ties and comprehension of God's Word. When meaningfulness is established, children realize why they're learning God's Word. It's during the stage of Roses that children begin nurturing a deeper understanding of God's truth, His will, and His plan of salvation.

Say you were instructed to memorize the following series of numbers: 3792118. Your initial response would no doubt be, "Why?" You'd question the relevancy of learning seemingly worthless numbers. Even if you were informed that these were the numbers to Joe Shmoe's phone number, you'd still not care to learn them—unless Joe was a personal friend. Just assigning relevancy such as "phone number" is meaningless. *Personal relevancy* is the key that makes something worth memorizing. As educators and parents, we want to instill personal relevancy of God's Word in our children—to help them understand that God's Word has direct meaning in their lives today and for all their tomorrows. Once children realize that Scripture is relevant in their own lives, they'll memorize the Word more quickly and easily!

The Roses step may be remembered by the love and understanding associated with God's Word. For example, guiding children to feel the emotion of John 3:16 will help them recall the verse more easily. God has so much love for the world that He gave the most precious gift anyone could give—His Son! Help your child understand the love behind the gift by asking questions such as "What's the most special present you'd give someone?" "How do you feel when you give someone a special gift?" "How does that person feel when a gift is received?" By helping children create emotional ties with this verse, they will understand how much mightier God's gift of Jesus was than a new doll or toy truck. They will begin to understand the depth of the verse. Emotion draws children closer to God and develops personal relevancy.

The goals in memorizing God's Word include repeating His Word (tulips) and understanding what God's Word is telling us (roses). But an important final blossom must be gathered before long-term memory occurs—the blossom of *Forget-Me-Nots*.

Roses create memorable feelings and impressions. Hep children to feel God's Word in memorable and connected ways!

STEP 3: FORGET-ME-NOTS (application)

"I will not neglect your word" (Psalm 119:16). By far the most time consuming teaching step in the Scripture Bouquet, is the *Forget-Me-Not*s step—and is meant to last a lifetime. Where recitation and comprehension quickly allow Scripture to enter the heart and mind, repetition affixes it to that "top drawer" of long-term memory. Frequent review, reinforcement, and enrichment help children keep the verses they've learned alive and ready to recall.

Set aside a regular review time each week. You'll not only be helping children remember what they've learned, but it's a great refresher for your own memory as well! Make both verbal recitation and brief discussions of specific verses part of your review sessions, then spend the remainder of the time with enriching games and other activities that are outlined in the next portion of this book.

Memorizing Scripture as a family not only bonds you to God's Word, it strengthens family bonds as well. Look for times to "quiz" each other on verses and their meanings whether at church, at home—or even washing the car!

TRY THIS!

Have kids decorate index cards with a verse on one side and the chapter and verse number on the flip side. Take turns quizzing each other on the verses, references, and meanings of the verses.

Do you have a mental picture of the Scripture Bouquet; of each flower and what it represents in the stages of Scripture memory? You've just demonstrated the effective use of *mnemonics*. The next part of this chapter will deal with mnemonics; what they are and how they work for children (and adults!) to create powerful strategies for memorization.

Blossoms in the Scripture Bouquet

Tulips (oral recitation)

Rosess (understanding)

Forget-Me-Nots (application)

> *I have hidden your word in my heart....*
> —Psalm 119:11

Chapter Four

WHAT IS MNEMONICS?

Mnemonics (pronounced "ne-MON-ix") can best be defined as the use of memory aids. Like much of our English language, the word mnemonics has its origins in ancient Greek mythology and the Greek goddess "Mnemosyne" whose realm was memory. Mnemonic techniques date back to about 500 BC when Greek scholars searched for help in memorizing long oratories.

The study of mnemonics is fascinating and there are as many mnemonic techniques and strategies for memorization as there are people to memorize. What differentiates mnemonics from learning strategies or styles (such as visual, concrete, auditory, and kinesthetic learning), is that mnemonics have relatively little to do with the information being memorized. Take for example our Scripture Bouquet and the mnemonic techniques for remembering each flowery step. Tulip flowers have nothing to do with oral recitation—but creating a play on the word "tulips" to derive "two lips" helps us remember that this step deals with lips—voice—and hence, recitation. Mnemonics, then, is imposing structure or meaning to what we wish to memorize.

Mnemonic techniques may be visual or verbal (including auditory). Visual mnemonics create scenes or images in the mind to help create associations between those images and the words you're memorizing. Verbal and auditory mnemonics are strategies which use words or sounds (which include rhyme, song, and rhythm) to help spur memory recognition.

MNEMONIC CLUES

VISUAL	VERBAL
Visual mnemonics create scenes or images in the mind to create associations between images and words. For example, to remember the words "for God so loved the world," you might visualize God embracing the world in a huge hug. Concrete visuals such as physical objects or pictures provide children with picture clues to spur recollection of verses. Isaiah 53:6 is a good example where using pictures of sheep help children remember that "we all, like sheep, have gone astray."	Verbal and auditory mnemonics use words or sounds to spur memory recognition. Songs that sequentially incorporate the books of the Old or New Testaments are good example of verbal mneumonics.

You've no doubt acquired your own repertoire of active mnemonics and aren't even aware of them. Some of the following examples are common mnemonic devises and may include ones you're familiar with.

- The difference between stalactites and stalagmites: Stalactites hold "tight" from cave ceilings. (Verbal mnemonics.)
- How to spell dessert and desert: Dessert is **s**weet **s**tuff (double "s") and desert is sand (one "s"). (Visual mnemonics.)
- Which is the left hand and which is the right: Hold your hands as if you're wearing mittens. The hand that makes the "L" is the left hand. (Visual mnemonics.)
- The color order of rainbows: ROY G. BIV: Red, Orange, Yellow, Green, Blue, Indigo, and Violet. (Visual mnemonics.)
- When Columbus discovered America: "Columbus sailed the ocean blue in fourteen hundred and ninety two." (Verbal mnemonics.)

Mnemonic devises or strategies are especially helpful when you create your own. Personal meaning creates strong memory attachments to mnemonics and studies have proven that self-created mnemonics rarely leave the memory.

Now let's put the important information we've been gathering in the last few chapters to practical use. In the following pages, you'll see how short-term memory, long-term memory, and mnemonics all work to create seven, **Super Strategies** for locking Scripture deep in children's hearts and minds—and how to bring forth the Word for a lifetime!

STRATEGY 1: LETTERING

Lettering is a visual mnemonic strategy and includes the use of alphabetizing, spelling, and alliteration. Looking for "unusual" letters such as q's or z's or x's in a verse, noting lists of words that may be placed in natural or reverse order of the alphabet, or hearing repetitive letter sounds all work to create great memory aids!

- **A-B-C order.** What could be more natural to a young child than the simplicity of the A-B-C's? School-aged children know the alphabet and with this knowledge are able to look for words that may be placed in alphabetical order—or in kid-terms: A-B-C order. How does this work? Look at the following shapes and suppose for a moment you were told to memorize their order for a type of circuit board.

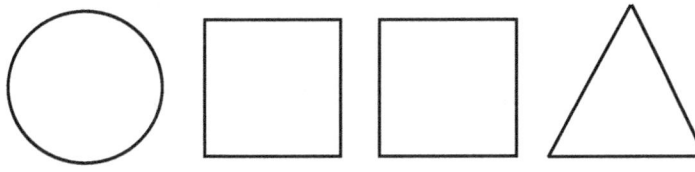

I have hidden your word in my heart....
—Psalm 119:11

Chapter Four

Your strategy, using A-B-C order, would be to say the name of each shape noting the beginning letter of each. You'd have a pattern of C-S-S-T. Notice how the shapes happen to be in sequential A-B-C order? Now the pattern is simple to recall! Apply this same strategy to the following verse. "Your word is a lamp to my feet and a light to my path" (Psalm 119:105). Young children typically forget which comes first: the *light* or the *lamp*? The path or the feet? By using the Lettering Strategy (A-B-C order), this verse becomes a snap! Since the "l-a" in lamp comes alphabetically before the "l-i" in light, children remember that "lamp" comes before "light" in the verse. It's the same with "feet" and "path" ("f" comes before "p" in the alphabet). Couple this with visual mnemonics or imagery where you carry a "lamp for your feet" to see the "light on the path." After using this strategy, few children stumble over this verse again!

Reverse A-B-C order also works well. In the following verse, note the reverse order of the underlined words. "Jesus answered, "I am the way and the truth and the life. No one comes to the Father except through me" " (John 14:6). The words "way," "truth," and "life" (w, t, l) appear in reverse A-B-C order.

Kids love looking for word patterns as they read. Even first grade children are learning alphabetical order and rhyming words.

When you point out A-B-C- order to your child, it's best to write out the verse, then invite your child to circle the key words or letters with a colorful marker. The Lettering Strategy is especially effective when coupled with a visual sentence. Most children will actually "see" the letter order of words as a verse is repeated verbally from that point on.

✦ *Alliteration.* "She sells sea shells by the sea shore." This may be a real tongue twister, but it's also a marvelous illustration of alliteration. Alliteration is best defined as a series of words all beginning with the same letter sound. It's an effective technique often used in children's literature and advertising where you hear pitches like, "Big Bert's Beans 'N Bacon can't be beat!" Alliteration is catchy and cute, heavenly to hear, really rad to repeat—and makes memory-magic. It's no wonder this lettering strategy is especially effective in Scripture memory with children! Many verses in Scripture contain alliteration. Here are a couple of excellent examples:

> "Because your love is better than life, my lips will glorify you" (Psalm 63:3).

> "And we have seen and testified that the Father has sent his Son to be the Savior of the world" (1 John 4:14).

36

Look for alliteration in verses you're memorizing and be sure to write the verses out and let your child circle the words that begin with the same letters. Then encourage your child to visualize those letters and words as he or she repeats the verse aloud.

STRATEGY 2: LUMPING.

In his book "Your Memory: How It Works and How to Improve It," Dr. Kenneth L. Higbee refers to one powerful memory strategy as chunking or lumping. Lumping is taking a large portion and breaking it into smaller, more manageable pieces. Children typically learn the letters of the alphabet through the lumping technique. Sing the Alphabet Song as you look at the letters below.

> *AB—CD—EFG*
> *HI—JK—LMNOP*
> *QRS—TUV—WX—Y and Z*

Notice how the letters are in small groups or lumps? Now repeat the alphabet in a slow, steady rhythm. It sounds strange and may even be a little difficult to repeat without lumping the letters. This is a good illustration of how material learned through lumping remains planted in your memory longer and may even become a natural part of recall.

Memorizing Acts 4:12 was a veritable battle for the 9- to 12-year-olds in my Bible class—until I applied the Lumping Strategy! "Salvation is found in no one else, for there is no other name under heaven given to men by which we must be saved." Here's how we broke down this challenging verse:

Lump 1: "Salvation is found in no one else…
Lump 2: for there is no other name under heaven…
Lump 3: given to men…
Lump 4: by which we must be saved."

As a group, the children noted that the word "no" is used in the first two lumps. We also implemented rhythm in lump 4 by stressing the following underlined words: "by <u>which</u> we <u>must</u> be <u>saved</u>." It worked beautifully and the children never stumbled over this verse again! Lumping strategies used by themselves or in conjunction with rhythm or song work to create long-term memory retention and recall.

STRATEGY 3: PATTERNING

If you find structure or organized patterns in what you're learning, chances are you'll remember it. Patterns in Scripture verses may include: repetition of particular words or phrases, antonyms (opposite words), and synonyms

I have hidden your word in my heart…. —Psalm 119:11

(similar words). Pointing out patterns or encouraging your child to find his or her own system of patterns, is an effective memory strategy in verse memorization. Here are some good examples:

"For I am convinced that neither death nor life, neither angels nor demons, neither the present nor the future, nor any powers, neither height nor depth, nor anything else in all creation, will be able to separate us from the love of God that is in Christ Jesus our Lord." (Romans 8:38,39)

STRATEGY: There are four sets of opposite words in this verse—death/life, angels/demons, present/future, and height/depth. There is also word repetition—"nor" is repeated six times and always separates the antonyms.

"Therefore, if anyone is in Christ, he is a new creation; the old has gone, the new has come!" (2 Corinthians 5:17)

STRATEGY: Opposite words: gone/come and new/old; the pattern is "new—old/gone—new/come." Point out that when something is old, we want to toss it out and have it gone. But when something is new it's just arrived or come!

"Love does not delight in evil but rejoices with the truth. It always protects, always trusts, always hopes, always perseveres. Love never fails." (1 Corinthians 13:6-8)

STRATEGY: There are a variety of patterning strategies at work here. Repetition of the word "always" is perhaps the most obvious. There are also two sets of near opposites: evil/truth and always/never. It's also important to point out that the first and last sentences begin with the word "love." Write out this verse portion for older children and allow them to use colored felt tips to draw hearts around the patterns they find. This technique provides visual reinforcement of patterns and allows children to visualize the sentences in the verse as they repeat them.

The use of patterning as a memory strategy is not only effective, but offers children great fun. Encourage children to be Scripture detectives and search for patterns in letters, words, and phrases!

STRATEGY 4: LISTING

Noting lists of people, places, objects, emotions, or verbs in a Scripture verse can effectively lock that verse in a child's mind and heart. The key is in linking the items in a list together. Dr. Kenneth Higbee gives a wonderful example of how listing works in memorizing the Ten Commandments. To remember the Ten Commandments you might link the following words together:

One God, graven idol, swearing, Sabbath, parents, kill, adultery, steal, lie, covet. Forming mental images of each link in the list cements the Commandments in memory: One God tossing out a graven idol; someone swearing outside a church (church representing the Sabbath); parents killing a mosquito on their child's arm; a married couple stealing a wedding ring; and a person lying about wanting their neighbor's sports car.

Visual images linked with key words from a list create powerful memory aids! Allow your child to count the items in the list, then draw the items to provide a concrete visual memory map that is structured and facilitates recall. Here is an example of how listing works in a particular Scripture verse.

"All Scripture is God-breathed and is useful for: teaching, rebuking, correcting and training in righteousness, so that the man of God may be thoroughly equipped for every good work." (2 Timothy 3:16,17)

STRATEGY: First break the verse into lumps as follows:
Lump 1: "All Scripture is God-breathed and is useful for…
Lump 2: teaching, rebuking, correcting and training in righteousness…
Lump 3: so that the man of God may be equipped for every good work.

Next, notice the list in the second lump. Create a mental image or concrete drawing of something that links the four underlined items, such as a teacher in training clothes shaking a finger while rebuking and correcting the class. Through lumping, visual imagery, and listing, this verse becomes easier. And when coupled with a discussion of what the verse means, children are more likely to remember the verse over time.

Before we tackle strategies 5, 6, and 7, it's important to point out that any of these memory strategies is solid in and of itself but works best when presented in combination with others strategies and teachings that help children comprehend the verse. The key is in finding an effective combination of strategies for the particular verse you're memorizing—and coupling it with reinforcement.

STRATEGY 5: VISUALIZING

To coin an old telephone commercial, visualizing is the "next best thing to being there." It creates concrete emotions and structured scenes where there are only abstracts. Imagine a sultry summer night when stars are glittering and moonbeams bathe a meadow glen. A small freckled fawn stands in the moonlight silently nibbling tender shoots. Do the words paint a picture or forge a feeling? Visual imagery by itself is not totally effective—but when it creates an association with an emotion or feeling, visualization becomes a powerful memory aid for children.

To make visual association most effective in your children, the imagery must be interactive in nature. You can think of this interaction as the difference

I have hidden your word in my heart…
—Psalm 119:11

between a still-life photograph and an action movie scene. For example, a child will recall the scene of Moses parting the Red Sea more completely and emotionally if he views the movie "The Ten Commandments" rather than seeing a painted caricature of Moses standing beside still waters. Encourage children to paint mental pictures of Scripture illustrating the emotion, setting, and circumstance of each verse. When the pictures have been thoroughly "painted," ask questions to increase and clarify understanding of the verse, encouraging your child to completely experience the words. Steer clear of "yes" and "no" questions and pose queries which require contemplation and feeling such as, "Why do think that…?" "What might have happened if…" "How do we know that…?" and "How does it make you feel?" Helping children memorize Scripture isn't by word alone—it requires meaning and emotion which facilitate verbal recall and enable children to apply God's Word in their lives!

> D. W. Kee and S. Y. Nakayama conducted studies in children's memory (Encoding in Children's Memory, 1980) and clinically proved that kindergarten aged children memorized phrases and items more completely and with greater recall when interactive visualizing was used.

STRATEGY 6: SINGING, RHYTHM 'N RHYME

There's only one thing more joyful than a song on the lips—God's Word in the heart! Children love song, rhythm, and rhyme and with a few word changes, familiar tunes become potent Scripture memory enhancers. Simply choose a familiar rhyme or tune that works with the particular verse you're memorizing. For example, try singing Luke 1:37 to the tune of "Ten Little Indians."

"For noth-ing is im-poss-i-ble with our God…
"For noth-ing is im-poss-i-ble with our God…
"For noth-ing is im-poss-i-ble with our God,"
Luke, one thir-ty sev-en.

This verse makes a nice song for children and one you'll readily pick up, too! Turn into creative "composers" and encourage children to put verses to music. The next portion of this book even provides you with fun musical instruments to make and use while joyfully singing God's Word.

Here's a list of public domain songs that are familiar to almost all children. Use them to help put Scripture into song.

- "Ten Little Indians"
- "Row, Row, Row Your Boat"
- "Mulberry Bush"
- "London Bridge"
- "This Old Man"
- "Three Blind Mice"
- "Frere Jacques"
- "God Is So Good"
- "Jesus Loves Me"
- "Did You Ever See a Lassie?"
- "Farmer in the Dell"
- "Old MacDonald Had a Farm"

> A lovely gift for a parent or grandparent is a tape recording of a beautiful "Scripture Concert" sung by their child. It's guaranteed to become a treasured keepsake and a wonderful way to put a song in Grandma's or Grandpa's heart!

Rhythm and rhyme are siblings of song. Remember those old nursery rhymes you learned as a child? There was Little Miss Muffet and her tuffet, Jack be nimble and his infamous candlestick, and who could forget Humpty Dumpty (poor egghead!)? Practically no one if they recited those rhymes in childhood and repeated them later to their children. What makes these often silly little ditties stick like glue to long-term memory? Repetition, rhythm, and rhyme! The snappy, catchy combination of words put to a definite rhythm make nursery rhymes fun to learn, delightful to say, and easy to recall. Couldn't we apply the same principles to Scripture memory? Try this one from Philippians 4:13…

> **I-can-DO** (clap)
> **ev'rything-THROUGH** (clap)
> **Him-who-gives-me-STRENGTH!** (clap, clap)

Kids of all ages love singing, rapping, chanting, or playing musical instruments in time to the "beat" of different verses!

Obviously not every verse in Scripture easily fits into rhythm, rhyme, or song, especially if the verse is lengthy. But there are many verses which lend themselves well to this mnemonic tool, and—

they're powerfully effective from the start and lock God's Word in mind and heart!

I have hidden your word in my heart….
—Psalm 119:11

Chapter Four

STRATEGY 7: MANIPULATIVES

Technically, the use of *concrete manipulatives* is not considered a mnemonic device, but I have included it here because of its great efficacy in helping young children memorize Scripture. I remember using tiny sour-ball candies when the children in my Bible class were having a two-fold problem: learning Luke 6:45 ("The good man brings good things out of the good stored up in his heart, and the evil man brings evil things out of the evil stored up in his heart. For out of the overflow of his heart his mouth speaks"), and battling negative talk about their friends. Clearly, the children needed a concrete example of this verse to help them learn the Scripture and understand and apply it in their lives. After reading Luke 6:45, I handed each child a colorful candy ball—so innocent and inviting. But what they expected to be sweet on their tongues turned out to be unpleasantly sour. Here was my opening!

Using concrete objects and pictures that children see, feel, taste, and smell help make Scripture verses come alive and are invaluable in aiding memory.

Try using a birthday cake and small gifts to learn John 3:16, Luke 2:11, or a host of others about Christ's birth or God's gift of salvation!

We talked of how words are affected by the condition of our hearts—that if people are feeling mean and given to gossip, slander, and negativity, it would come forth from their mouths, like the sour taste of the candy. We reread Luke 6:45 and read Matthew 15:11 and the children began to see that only appearing to be sweet like candy was a sour lie that Jesus sees through! They not only learned the verse word for word, but had an immediate change in behavior and speech. Thank you, God, for your precious Word!

Taste honey to help children remember Psalm 19:10, feel sheep's fleece to experience Isaiah 53:6, or smell incense to help children learn and remember Psalm 141:2. Look for verses that will powerfully lend themselves to the use of concrete manipulatives—and watch that Scripture stick!

We've reached the end of our discussion on memory and memory-making strategies for helping children memorize God's Word. But it's really just the beginning! In the second half of this book you'll discover lively activities, games, songs, and much more to motivate, introduce, teach, reinforce, and enrich Scripture for children. God bless you as you seek to fill children's lives—and your own—with the power and fullness of God's Word.

> **"Teach them to your children, talking about them when you sit at home and when you walk along the road, when you lie down and when you get up" (Deuteronomy 11:19).**

I have hidden your word in my heart....
—Psalm 119:11

Chapter Five

3- to 6-Year-Olds

Can anytime be brighter in a child's life than being an energetic toddler through the first year of "big kids' school"? Three- to six-year-olds are filled with imagination, discovering the joys of first friendships, engaged in helping others while maintaining a sense of autonomy when it comes to being helped. The three- to six-year-old is bright, emotional, and very eager to learn—*anything!* The whole world is new and exciting, and their senses are 100% alive!

Tasting, touching, hearing, smelling, and seeing are the fundamental ways a young child responds to and learns from his surrounding world. Because of a limited—but growing—vocabulary, abstract concepts and explanations are lost to the merrier pursuits of concrete pictures, songs, and hands-on activities. Three- to six-year-olds want to explore their worlds and need to experience their worlds. Teaching must be geared toward solid, concrete techniques involving hands-on games, pictures and activities, snappy enough to hold wandering interests and lightening fast attention spans! Zero in on that old teacher's adage:

IF I HEAR, I FORGET.
IF I SEE, I LEARN.
IF I DO, I UNDERSTAND!

God's Word is fundamental to hear, important to see, but vital to understand! Allow your three- to six-year-olds to actively "do" while learning Scripture, and they will grow in memorizing God's Word and begin to nurture solid understanding of what Scripture says. Since the attention spans of children in this age level range from rounds per millisecond to rounds per minute, don't set high expectations for lengthy Scripture sessions! Instead, set aside two 5-minute Scripture sessions a week and invite quick reviews once or twice daily. Nurturing a lifestyle of love for and learning God's Word begins in early childhood and spans a lifetime. Help young children weave God's Word into their lives as a natural, pleasurable part of their Christian faith!

The activities in the following pages are presented in age appropriate ways for three- to six-year-old children. Mix and match them according to your children's interests and abilities and allow flexibility in adapting these tools to the particular verses you've chosen to memorize or review. Remember to use a variety of ideas at regular intervals to reinforce and review verses you've already learned!

Each activity is divided into these sections:

➤ **Scripture Bouquet** (gives the memory step the activity is suited for)
➤ **Memory Strategy** (gives any mnemonic method used)
➤ **Supply List** (lists any items needed for activity)
➤ **Overview** (provides a quick look at the activity)
➤ **The Activity** (clear-cut directions, simple patterns, and helpful hints)

At the end of the section are reinforcement charts to motivate Scripture learning and to promote routine review. Keep multiple photocopies of these pages in a special folder and rotate them often to keep interest high. Make copies of the reinforcement pages for yourself and tape them alongside your children's pages as you strive to model the importance of Scripture memory in your own life.

Have fun! Make memories! And share in God's precious Word, learning its fullness together!

Jesus said, "Let the little children come to me." —Matthew 19:14

Scripture Bouquet Step:

Tulips;
Forget-Me-Nots

Memory Strategy:

Manipulatives;
Rebus pictures

Supplies:

* index cards
* markers
* crayons
* recipe card box (optional)

PICTURE THIS!

Verse: Any simple verses containing words that can be made into pictures

Overview: Rebus puzzles use pictures in place of certain words in a sentence. They are great fun for young Scripture scholars and offer help in reading simple verses as well as providing pictures clues that strengthen recall.

The Activity

Choose a verse that contains words that can be easily illustrated, for example: a picture of a **knot** for the word "not," a **sun** for the word "Son," or a **needle and thread** for the word "so." Use markers and crayons to write the verse and draw pictures in place of certain words on one side of an index card. Write the Scripture reference on back of the card and draw a picture clue from the verse.

Take turns "reading" your rebus Scripture cards aloud. Then play Fun Flash by showing the verse reference and picture clue to children. Encourage them to repeat the verse on the other side. Decorate recipe card boxes and keep your rebus Scripture cards handy for frequent practice.

Try these verses using Rebus pictures:
• John 3:16
• John 6:35
• John 11:35
• Romans 3:16

SCRAMBLED EGGS

Verse: Any simple verse (or verse portion)

Overview: Egg hunts are such fun! But these eggs are different. Hidden inside each are words to a Scripture verse. Find the eggs, then put the words together to make the verse.

The Activity

Write words or lumped phrases to a verse on the slips of paper. Place each slip of paper inside a plastic egg, then hide the eggs. Invite your child to go on an egg hunt and collect the eggs. Then have your child open the eggs and reconstruct the Scripture verse. Read it aloud, then replace the papers inside the eggs. Have your child hide the eggs for you this time. When you're finished, tape the verse together and hang it on a door or wall to be reread often.

TRY THIS!

This game is especially fun as a classroom relay race for slightly plder kids. Use two sets of eggs and hide them in separate areas of the room. Have groups A and B hunt for their eggs and reconstruct the verse. End with a jellybean hunt for everyone!

Scripture Bouquet Step:

Tulips;
Roses

Memory Strategy:

Visualizing;
Lumping

Supplies:

* plastic pull-apart eggs
* markers
* slips of paper
* scissors
* tape
* glitter glue & paper confetti (optional)

Scripture Bouquet Step:

Tulips;
Forget-Me-Nots

Memory Strategy:

Manipulatives;
Lumping; Games

Supplies:

* markers
* scissors
* metal paper clips
* self-adhesive magnetic strips
* string or yarn
* a yardstick
* tape

SCRIPTURE FISH

Verse: "Come follow me," Jesus said, "and I will make you fishers of men" (Matthew 4:19), or any verse you want to review.

Overview: This fun game combines "fishing" and Scripture practice. Use the above verse or any verse you wish to fish for!

The Activity

Photocopy the five fish shapes from the facing page onto stiff paper, then cut them out. Invite children to color the paper fish using markers. Slide a metal paper clip on the mouth of each fish and tape it in place. Cut a 3-foot length of string or yarn and tie one end to a long stick. On the opposite end of the string, tie or tape a piece of self-adhesive magnetic tape.

If you are working to learn Matthew 4:19, write a few words on the back of each fish until you've written the verse and reference. (If you're using the fish to review other verses, simply write the verses—or portions of the verses—on slips of paper. Tape the slips to the backs of the fish.)

Take turns "fishing" to catch the paper fish. (The paper clips will stick to the magnetic strip on the fishing line.) After the fish are reeled in, help children construct the verse, then read it aloud several times before fishing again. For very young children, omit writing the verse on the backs of the fish. When a fish is caught, lead your child in repeating the verse, then catch another and repeat the verse again.

Even toddlers love fishing—but they enjoy spending time with loving caregivers more! Share time in learning God's Word *together* every day!

Make a verse mobile using the fish shapes. Write verses you've learned on each fish, then suspend them from a clothes hanger.

Fish Patterns

Permission to photocopy for church, school, or home use only. Taken from *Scripture Memory Makers*
© Susan Lingo, Susan Lingo Books, 2007.

Scripture Bouquet Step:

Roses;
Forget-Me-Nots

Memory Strategy:

Manipulatives

Supplies:

* plastic bowl
* colorful permanent markers
* paint pens
* newspapres

EACH DAY GOD'S WAY

Verse: Any simple verse you choose to learn or review

Overview: Using common items such as table setting, dishes, or comb and brushes offer everyday reinforcement of verses you're working to learn!

The Activity

Spread newspapers on a table or over the floor. Place colorful permanent markers and paint pens on the paper. (Let children know that "permanent" markers will stay on their skin, so be careful. We want God's Word permanently in heart and mind—but not marker on hands!)

Help children write the verse you've chosen to learn or reinforce on the sides of each plastic bowl. Then invite children to use the markers and paint pens to decorate the sides of the bowls. Simple designs such as heart or flower shapes, swirls, zigzags, and dots work well.

TRY THIS! Try adding verses using permanent markers or paint pens to the following items for everyday use and reinforcement:

• plastic tumblers
• wide flatware handles
• backs of hair brushes
• vinyl placemats
• toothbrush handles

As children work, remind them that God desires us to work each day to learn His Word. Seeing pictures and the verse on the plastic bowl each day will help children recall the verse you've chosen. Challenge children to repeat the verse out loud each time they use their special Scripture bowls.

TEAR TRIANGLES

Verse: "Jesus wept" (John 11:35) or Psalm 119:28, Jeremiah 31:13b, or any dealing with tears, sadness, or sorrow turned to joy

Overview: This is the shortest verse in Scripture yet creates the deepest emotion. Use this concrete craft project to help young children starting to memorize God's Word understand that Jesus felt sadness even though He loved us so greatly.

The Activity

Mix a few drops of blue food coloring in a small bowl of water, then set it aside. After you've encouraged children to repeat the verse a few times, ask questions such as, "What do we do when we're really sad?" "Why do you think Jesus cried?" "What would you have said to Jesus to make Him feel better?"

Invite children to dribble blue "tear drops" on sheets of waxed paper using an eye dropper. Fold paper towels or coffee filters into triangular shapes, then have children dab the "tear drops" with the corners of the paper. Carefully open the papers and look at the pretty designs made by the "tear drops." Explain that even though Jesus cried, He felt great joy in loving us. Hang the tear-triangles on a wall and encourage your child to touch the "tears" and repeat the verse each time they pass by.

TERRIFIC TIP ✓
Cut paper towels or coffee filters in half for smaller, but easier-to-absorb, designs. Use markers to write the verse on the papers.

Scripture Bouquet Step:

Roses

Memory Strategy:

Visualizing

Supplies:

✹ food coloring

✹ bowls of water

✹ paper towels or coffee filters

✹ waxed paper

✹ eye dropper

RHYTHM RIBBONS

Scripture Bouquet Step:

Tulips

Memory Strategy:

Rhythm 'n Rhyme

Supplies:

* 1-inch wide ribbon
* scissors
* small stickers (optional)

Verse: "And this is what he promised us—even eternal life" (1 John 2:25), "We all, like sheep, have gone astray…" (Isaiah 53:6), or any other verses that contain a strong, rhythmic beat.

Overview: Let young child feel the joyous rhythm in this verse with a promise. It's Scripture to celebrate!

The Activity

Cut two 10-inch lengths of colored ribbon for each child, then set the ribbon aside. Repeat one of the Scripture verses as follows, clapping on the upper case words. Repeat the verse three times, then encourage children to repeat it with you.

"We ALL, like SHEEP, have GONE astray…" ISAIAH 53:6.

"And THIS is WHAT he PRO-MISED us…EVEN e-TER-nal LIFE" FIRST JOHN, two-twenty-FIVE.

Gently tie ribbons to the index fingers of the children. Have children "finger clap" by tapping their ribboned fingers together on the beats of the verse. Mention that people often tie strings or ribbons around their fingers to help them remember important things. Remind children that we want to remember God's Word, and the ribbons will help. Encourage children to create new rhythm patterns for the verses, then use "finger clapping" to clap out the rhythms while reciting the Scripture verse and reference.

Preschool children respond to music, rhythm, and rhyme. Look for ways to match verses with short tunes or lively rhythms.

TRY THIS!

Use your rhythm ribbons as bookmarks for Bibles. Personalize the ribbons with colorful stickers.

I CAN LEARN!

Verse: "I can do everything through him who gives me strength" (Philippians 4:13)

Overview: Help young child realize they *can* learn, understand, and use God's Word—and that Jesus will help!

The Activity

Remove the top lid from each can as well as the label. (Prepare one can for each child.) Photocopy the can label at the bottom of this page on white paper, one per child. Invite children to color the labels using markers or crayons then cut out the labels. Help children glue the labels to the fronts of the empty cans.

As you work, tell children that canned goods contain foods that help us grow and become healthy—just as God's Word does for our hearts, minds, and souls. Explain that because God desires us to learn, understand, and use His Word, He helps us. In fact, through Jesus, we can do *all* things—including learning Scripture! Read the label to children and point out the words to Philippians 4:13. Ask children what other things God and Jesus help us do. Then repeat the verse three more times. Keep verse cards in the cans for quick reviews.

Scripture Bouquet Step:

Tulips; Roses

Memory Strategy:

Manipulatives

Supplies:

* clean soup can
* markers
* crayons
* scissors
* glue or clear packing tape
* copies of the can label from this page

GOOD-FRUIT BASKET

Scripture Bouquet Step: Forget-Me-Nots

Memory Strategy: Lumping; Manipulatives

Supplies:
* markers
* crayons
* scissors
* tape
* baskets
* copies of the fruit patterns

Verse: Any simple verse you choose to learn or review

Overview: Manipulatives add motivation to memory practice. Use the patterns on the following three pages (or use plastic fruit). Then be the first to fill a basket with the fruit of God's Word.

The Activity

Before this activity, photocopy the fruit patterns on stiff paper and cut out the patterns. Write the verse or verse portions you wish to review on the backs of the paper fruit. Invite children to color the fruit as they desire.

Have children hide their eyes as you place the pieces of fruit around the room. Hand a basket to each player. (If you have a large group, form pairs and hand each pair a basket.)

On "go," have players hunt for the pieces of fruit and place them in their baskets. When a complete verse is found, have the child say, "I have the fruit of God's Word!" Then invite that player to hide the paper fruits for the next round of play.

TRY THESE IDEAS!

- Use plastic or wax fruit and on them tape slips of paper with the verses or verse portions written on them.
- Use this activity to help young children learn the *Fruit of the Spirit* from Galatians 5:22, 23. List a different spiritual fruit on each piece of paper fruit.
- After hiding and hunting paper fruit several times, serve fruit slices with yogurt dip for a refreshing snack!

54

Fruit Patterns

Permission to photocopy for church, school, or home use only.
Taken from *Scripture Memory Makers* © Susan Lingo,
Susan Lingo Books, 2007.

Fruit Patterns

Permission to photocopy for church, school, or home use only. Taken from *Scripture Memory Makers* © Susan Lingo, Susan Lingo Books, 2007.

Fruit Patterns

Permission to photocopy for church, school, or home use only. Taken from *Scripture Memory Makers* © Susan Lingo, Susan Lingo Books, 2007.

OUR LIFE SAVIOR

Scripture Bouquet Step:

Tulips;
Roses

Memory Strategy:

Lettering;
Manipulatives

Supplies:

* candy life-saver rings
* paper cups
* water

Verse: "The Father has sent his Son to be the Savior of the world" 1 John 4:14 or any verse with the word "Savior" in it.

Overview: With this "sweet" activity, help children understand that Jesus came to save our lives from sin and eternal death.

The Activity

Repeat the verse for children and point out the following "s" words: "sent," "Son," and "Savior." Explain that the words "Son" and "Savior" both refer to Jesus. Encourage children to repeat the verse three more times and listen for those special "S" words. As you say each word beginning with the letter sound of "S", have children either clap their hands or stand up then quickly sit back down. (Words to clap or pop up on are underlined in the verse below.)

*"The Father has **sent** his **Son** to be the **Savior** of the world."*

After repeating the verse several times, hand each child three candy life-saver rings and a small paper cup filled with water. Ask questions such as, "How can a life saver or life preserver help if you're drowning?" "What keeps you afloat in water?" Let children place one of their candies in the water. Point out how the candy life-saver ring floats. Explain that Jesus is like a life saver—He saves us from sin and gives us eternal life. Tell them that Jesus is our life saver or "Life Savior." Let children eat their candies, then repeat the Scripture verse reference three more times.

SCRIPTURE BALL

Verse: Any simple verse you choose to learn or review

Overview: This large motor game may be played indoors or out, and the inviting combination of quick action and oral repetition make it great for reviewing any Scripture verses!

The Activity

Have children form two lines facing each other. Take turns tossing or bouncing the ball back and forth between the lines and calling out a word to a Scripture verse with each toss. If the ball is dropped or someone misses a word, begin the verse again. Set a goal of three complete repetitions without missing a catch, then reward your practice time with a colorful, sugar-free gum ball or ball-shaped cookie for each player!

If you have very young children, have them sit on the floor in a circle and roll the ball to each other as they repeat the words to a simple verse.

TRY THIS!

For a challenging variation with slightly older children, form a standing circle with one child in the center. Hand the child in the center the ball and let him or her toss the ball high in the air and call out a reference for a verse the group has learned. Children run to catch the ball, then repeat the verse. Say a few words of the verse to get children started if they need help.

Kids of all ages love games using balls. Vary the kinds of balls you use to keep games fresh and exciting. Large beach balls are lightweight to toss and catch and small tennis balls are good for rolling. Challenge children to invent games using bouncy balls and Scripture to keep them bouncing closer to God!

Scripture Bouquet Step:
Forget-Me-Nots

Memory Strategy:
Games; Manipulatives

Supplies:

* a playground ball, soccer ball, or large beach ball

* sugar-free gumballs or ball-shaped cookies

MY SHADOW

Verse: "The Lord your God will be with you wherever you go" (Joshua 1:9).

Overview: This fun activity will help children see that God is like their protective, loving shadow who will always be with them.

The Activity

Before this activity, tape the sheet of poster board to the wall or a door. Write the Scripture verse on a separate sheet of paper in large letters. Read the verse and allow children to draw lines to separate the verse into the following lumps:

"The Lord your God"
"will be with you"
"wherever you go."

Point out a pattern in the verse by using the words "your" and "you": the verse lumps read: "your—you—you." Let children underline or circle those words in the verse, then invite volunteers to point to the words as the verse is repeated three more times.

Make a shadow on the poster board using a flashlight and your hands. Explain that just as a shadow is with us all the time, God is always with us, too. Point out that God is with us because He loves us. Encourage children to make shadows on the poster board to remind them of how God is with us and goes with us. Suggested shadow shapes might include a heart, walking fingers, two fingers held side-by-side, and prayer hands.

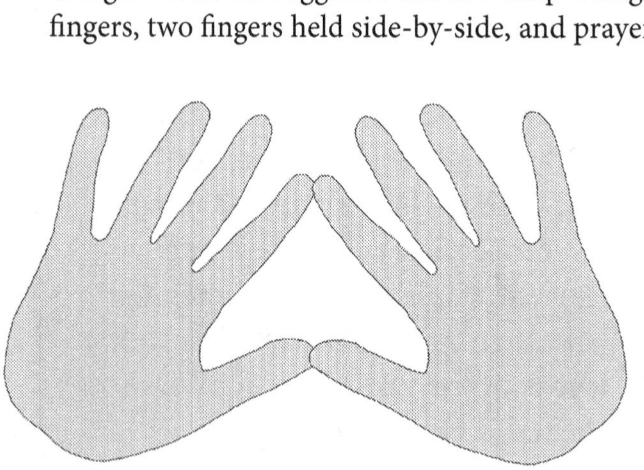

When everyone has had at least one turn to make shadows, challenge children to repeat the Scripture verse three more times as they make their shadow shape hearts on the sheet of poster board.

Scripture Bouquet Step:

Roses;
Forget-Me-Nots

Memory Strategy:

Patterning;
Lumping

Supplies:

✹ tape
✹ poster board
✹ markers
✹ paper
✹ flashlight

SCRIPTURE TOSS

Verse: Any simple verse you choose to learn or review

Overview: Tossing bean bags isn't just for carnival fun—it's a wonderful way to motivate children to practice Scripture verses!

The Activity

Before this activity, use markers to draw a four-ring target on a sheet of poster board. Color the inside circle of the target red, the next ring yellow, the next one orange, and the largest ring green. Make bean bags in a snap by pouring dried beans or uncooked rice into socks, then wrapping rubber bands around the ankle. Cut off excess material.

Repeat the verses you'll be reviewing and encourage children to say them aloud with you. Place the target on the floor and have children stand a few feet away. Take turns saying a verse then tossing the bean bags. Choose an M & M candy (or other small colored candy or cereal loop) that matches the color of the ring each bean bag lands on. Challenge children to see how many red and yellow candies they can collect in five tosses.

Young children find games of skill especially fun and challenging. Look for ways to combine skill games such as beanbag tosses, bowling, and basektball-type games with Scripture review.

Scripture Bouquet Step:

Tulips;
Forget-Me-Nots

Memory Strategy:

Manipulatives

Supplies:

✷ poster board

✷ markers

✷ clean socks

✷ scissors

✷ dried beans or uncooked rice

✷ rubber bands

✷ M&Ms candies

Scripture Bouquet Step:

Tulips;
Forget-Me-Nots

Memory Strategy:

Manipulatives

Supplies:

* paper lunch sacks
* markers
* crayons
* scissors
* copies of the verse cards
* glitter glue (optional)

VERSE PURSE

Verse: Any you wish to learn or review

Overview: Young children love making this colorful sack to keep their very own Scripture cards in—and to pull out for quick reviews, games, and reinforcement.

The Activity

Write "Verse Purse" across one side of each paper lunch sack. Photocopy the verse cards on the next page on stiff paper and cut them out. Prepare one set of verse cards for each child.

Invite children to decorate their paper purses as they desire. Designs might include stars to show how God made the world or hearts to symbolize our love for God. Use glitter glue to add sparkly touches if desired. Let children color the verse cards using crayons and markers.

For review: Place the verse cards in the floor in front of you. Hold up one of the cards and ask children to find the same card. Read the verse aloud and have children repeat the verse three times. Turn the card over, then read and repeat another verse. Continue until all of the verses have been reviewed and the cards are turned over. Have one child choose a card and read it aloud. Let the other children find the same card, repeat the verse, then place the cards in their Verse Purses. Continue until all of the cards are stored in the sacks.

TRY THIS! Use an old purse or wallet instead of the paper sacks.

For initial learning: Choose one card and verse to work on. Repeat the verse several times. (If there's a picture clue that works with this verse, draw that simple picture on the card to help aid in recall.) Tape the card to the outside top edge of the Verse Purse for quick review. When the verse is learned and can be repeated, place it in the sack to review later.

Verse Cards

Photocopy these cards on still paper then cut them out. Keep them in your Verse Purse and use them for learning, reviews, and games.

"His sheep follow him because they know his voice."

John 10:4

"But the fruit of the Spirit is love, joy, peace, patience, kindness, goodness, faithfulness, gentleness, and self-control…"

Galatians 5:22, 23

"I will make you fishers of men."

Matthew 4:19

"I can do everything through him who gives me strength."

Philippians 4:13

"The earth is the LORD's, and everything in it, the world, and all who live in it."

Psalm 24:1

"I am the good shepherd. The good shepherd lays down his life for the sheep."

John 10:11

Permission to photocopy for church, school, or home use only. Taken from *Scripture Memory Makers*
© Susan Lingo, Susan Lingo Books, 2007.

Scripture Bouquet Step:

Tulips;
Forget-Me-Nots

Memory Strategy:

Manipulatives;
Games

Supplies:

* markers
* scissors, glue
* poster board
* colored cereal loops
* paper slips
* photocopy of the game board on the facing page

SAY THAT VERSE!

Verse: Any you wish to learn or review

Overview: Even young children enjoy a lively board game—and combining the fun with learning God's Word is even better! This simple game invite you to "say-n-play" at the same time.

The Activity

Photocopy the game board on the facing page, then glue the sheet to poster board. (Color the game board using markers if desired.) Cut along the dotted lines and snip apart the playing cards. Choose a verse to learn or review and write it on a slip of paper. Place the slip of paper where all players can see it. Place colored cereal loops at "Start"—one per player. Turn the number and sheep cards face down.

To Play: Take turns drawing cards to see how many spaces you'll move. Follow the directions on the space you land on, repeating the verse on the slip of paper as directed. If a player chooses the card with the picture of the sheep, that player may choose someone to repeat the verse. Continue drawing cards until a player reaches "Home."

Spending time as a family learning Scripture, playing games, and sharing time makes God's Word even more memorable—and fun to learn!

As you play, explain to your child that knowing whom and what to follow is important. Tell your children that sheep will follow their shepherd because the shepherd guides the sheep to safety and cares for each one in the flock. Explain that God desires us to follow Him and follow His Word, too. That when we know God's Word and do as it says, it will keep us safe and living in God's will. Tell your children that learning to follow God's Word begins with knowing different verses—and that's why it's important to practice repeating God's Word.

MEMORY MOBILE

Scripture Bouquet Step:
Tulips

Memory Strategy:
Visualizing; Lumping

Supplies:
* markers
* construction paper
* scissors
* yarn or fishing line
* clear tape
* clothes hanger

Verse: Any simple verse you want to learn or review

Overview: Children love to watch the soothing, gentle motion of mobiles—especially ones they've made themselves! This Scripture memory craft is fun, easy, motivating, and adaptable to nearly any verse.

The Activity

Repeat the verse you're learning or reviewing three times, encouraging your child to repeat the verse with you. Help your child divide the verse into lumps or portions of words that are easier to remember. Cut that number of shapes from colorful construction paper using geometric shapes or shapes that represent words in the verse such a foot from Psalm 119:105 or prayer hands from 1 Thessalonians 5:17.

Write the words to each lump on the paper shapes, one portion per shape. Then cut varying lengths of yarn or fishing line. Tape each shape to one end and tape the other end of each to a coat hanger so that the words to the verse hang down in interesting ways—and in order, of course!

Encourage children to recite the verse again, pointing to the lumps as they repeat the verse. Tell children to hang their mobiles in places where they, and their whole family, can read the verse and repeat it often.

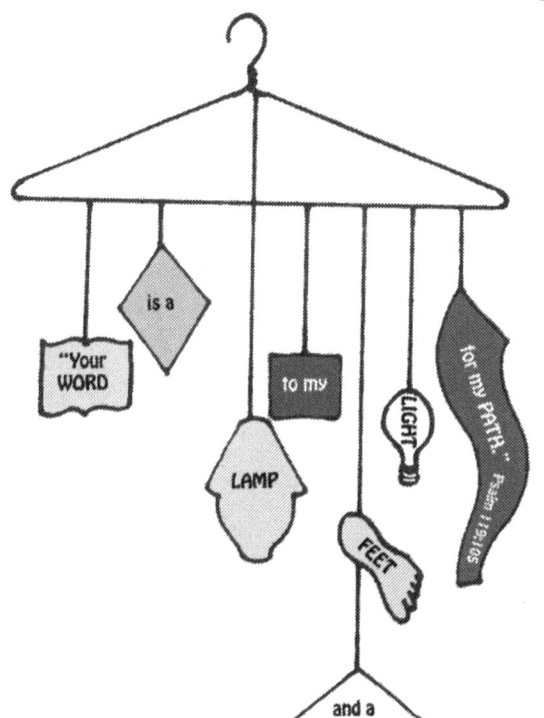

Other verses that work well visually and in lumps, include:

• John 3:16
• 1 Thessalonians 5:17
• John 6:35

HEART THROBS

Verse: "Love one another as I have loved you" (John 13:34).

Overview: Young children love rhythm instruments. Let them play with these fun, motivating drums—and help them memorize an important Scripture verse at the same time!

The Activity

Repeat the following verse three times stressing the underlined words in a rhythmic beat:

"<u>Love</u> one a-<u>noth</u>-er as <u>I</u> have loved <u>you</u>."

Ask children if they hear any pattern or rhythm in the words. Then lead children in repeating the verse three more times as they clap out the rhythm with the words.

Hand children each a paper or plastic cup. Invite them to decorate the cups using permanent markers. (Tell children to be careful not to get marker on their hands or clothing.) Help children stretch squares of plastic wrap tightly over the tops of the cups and secure them using rubber bands. When the tops of the cups are tapped with finger "drum sticks," they'll make wonderful sounds!

Lead children in making rhythmic "heart throbs" as they repeat the verse a few more times. Use your heart throb drums to rhythmically repeat verses they've previously learned

> If you're working on one specific verse, help children write the verse on the sides of the cups.

Scripture Bouquet Step:

Tulips

Memory Strategy:

Rhythm 'n Rhyme

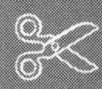

Supplies:

✷ paper or plastic cups

✷ plastic wrap

✷ rubber bands

✷ permanent markers

FROG JOG

Scripture Bouquet Step: Tulips; Forget-Me-Nots

Memory Strategy: Listing

Supplies:
* green construction paper
* scissors
* poster board
* markers
* tape
* copies of the frog & lily pad patterns

Verse: Any simple verse containing a list

Overview: Remember the fun in a good ol' fashioned game of Leap Frog? Frog Jog combines the fun of leap frog with the important reinforcement of Scripture repetition!

The Activity

Before this activity, photocopy the frog and lily pad patterns on stiff, green paper. (Use white paper if children would like to color the patterns themselves.) Cut out the patterns. Print the verse you're working to learn or reviewing on a sheet of poster board and tape it to the wall for everyone to see.

Lead children in repeating the verse two times, then point out the words in the list. (You may wish to circle these words.) Repeat the verse two more times.

TRY THIS! Make stick puppets by taping frog patterns to craft sticks, then leap over your partner's "pad" each time you say a word in a verse.

Have children get into pairs and hand a frog to one partner and a lily pad to the other. Position the "frogs" at one end of the room and the "lily pads" at the opposite end. Take turns repeating a word from the verse, then taking a leap or hop toward the other partner. Each item in the verse's "list" should constitute one leap. Challenge partners to meet in the middle of the room, frog on lily pad. Then exchange patterns and play again.

Games such as Leap Frog or Piggyback have their place in helping make Scripture memorable! Try a game of Leap Frog as partners repeat verses with lists.

Frog & Lily Pad

COLOR ME FUN

Scripture Bouquet Step:

Tulips; Forget-Me-Nots

Memory Strategy:

Games; Repetition

Supplies:

* markers
* scissors
* poster board
* glue
* construction paper
* slips of paper

Verse: Any you wish to learn or review—great for multiple verse review!

Overview: This colorful board game reinforces Scripture verses you've been working hard to learn—and colors memory work with a bit of fun.

The Activity

Photocopy the game board on the facing page, then glue the sheet to poster board. Color the game board and playing cards (following the color names) using bright markers. Cut apart the playing cards. Cut construction paper into small squares (using the colors listed on the game board and small enough to use as markers). Choose a verse to learn or review and write it on a slip of paper. Place the slip of paper where all players can see it. Set the pile of colored squares on the ark. Turn the color cards face down.

To Play: Take turns repeating the verse. When a player correctly repeats the verse, he draws a color card. Have that player place a colored square on the rainbow. Continue repeating the verse and drawing cards until the rainbow is complete.

As you play, explain that Noah obeyed God when he built the ark. Noah did just as God desired. Tell children that learning to say, understand, and use Scripture is what God desires of us, too—and that's why it's important to practice repeating God's Word.

PLAYING TIP

Instead of using poster board to back your game, glue it to one side of a large envelope. Keep playing pieces and color cards in the envelope for playing in a snap!

70

BLESSED "BEE" THE WORD

Photocopy this chart. Color the beehive and bees, then detach the gray strip of bees, and cut them. Write the verse you're learning or reviewing on the bee hive. Each time you review the verse, tape a bee flying closer and closer to the door of the hive. Place the last bee in the doorway. Save the finished page in a special folder for review.

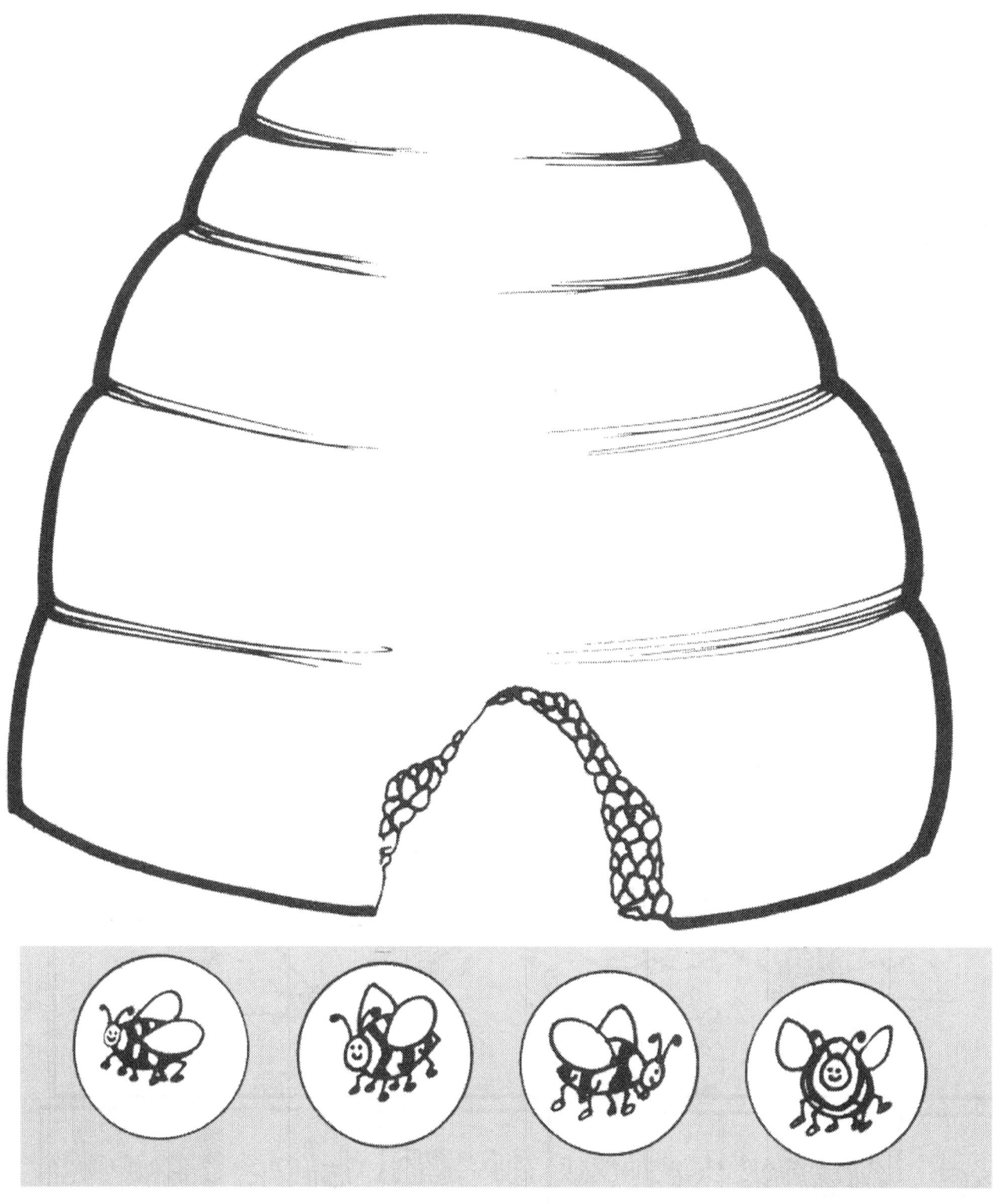

Permission to photocopy for church, school, or home use only. Taken from *Scripture Memory Makers*
© Susan Lingo, Susan Lingo Books, 2007.

BLOOM WITH GOD'S WORD!

Photocopy this page. Write the verse you're memorizing below the flower. Each time you practice the verse, color a flower petal on the page. When you're finished with the flower, save this page in a special folder for review.

Permission to photocopy for church, school, or home use only. Taken from *Scripture Memory Makers*
© Susan Lingo, Susan Lingo Books, 2007.

Chapter Six

7- to 12-Year-Olds

Eight- to twelve-year-olds are really on the grow! An increasing sense of autonomy fuels confidence and the desire to explore new vistas. A mixture of expanded vocabulary and cognitive reasoning work together to create a voracious appetite for *why* we do what we do. "*Why* do I have to learn this stuff in math?" "*Why* do I have to keep my room clean if I'm the only one living in it?" "*Why* am I learning God's Word and of what use is it in my life?" Of vital importance is creating a sense of personal relevance for God's Word in your child's life. Explain why Scripture is learned and memorized, clarify why Scripture is a powerful part of a Christian's life, and what having a ready command of God's Word can do. In other words, demonstrate an active-Scripture in your own life and how it helps you daily!

Though eight- to twelve-year-olds are at an age where newfound autonomy unfurls around them like a freedom-flag, they're also keenly aware of human judgment. Worries about "measuring up" and failing often create walls which begin showing stress fractures. We must be very careful never to give children the impression that memorizing Scripture is a win-fail contest. Explain that God's grace isn't measured by the number of verses we know—but just as grace is a gift from God, we can gift God in return by working to learn his Word.

Assure older children that missing a Scripture word here and there isn't going to make God angry or upset. God knows the desires of our hearts and He knows our intentions and promises to honor them. Read aloud Isaiah 55:11 to your child. *"…so is my word that goes out from my mouth: It will not return to me empty, but will accomplish what I desire and achieve the purpose for which I sent it."* Help children realize that when they try to memorize God's precious Word, He will honor their efforts—regardless of the number of verses they learn or how quickly they recall each word!

Older children have longer attention spans but are increasingly possessive of their time. They balk at anyone imposing restraints on what they do and when it's to be done! Allow children to help establish two 10-minute Scripture sessions weekly, then use extra moments at bedtime or in the car to reinforce verses you've learned.

Expanded cognition and higher-level reasoning create stimulating Scripture sessions with eight- to twelve-year-olds. Though they still enjoy hands-on learning techniques, more time must be spent in guiding comprehension of verses and motivating for reinforcement of Scripture they've already learned. The activities in the following section are age-appropriate ways to motivate children for review and reinforcement, and enrich comprehension of God's Word. Mix and match the activities according to your children's interests and allow flexibility in adapting these tools to the particular verse or verses you've chosen to memorize. Remember to use a variety of ideas at different times to review verses you've already learned!

Each activity is divided into these sections:

➤ **Scripture Bouquet** (gives the memory step the activity is suited for)
➤ **Memory Strategy** (gives any mnemonic method used)
➤ **Supply List** (lists any items needed for activity)
➤ **Overview** (provides a quick look at the activity)
➤ **The Activity** (clear-cut directions, simple patterns, and helpful hints)

At the end of this section are reinforcement pages to motivate Scripture study and to promote routine review. Keep multiple photocopies of these pages in a special folder and rotate them often to keep interest high. Make copies of the reinforcement pages for yourself and tape them alongside your child's pages to model the importance of Scripture memory. Be sure to check the three- to six-year-old section for additional activities and reinforcement charts you can adapt for older children. May God bless you and your children as you seek to learn, understand, and apply His powerful truths every day!

"Teach me knowledge and good judgment...." —Psalm 119:66

SCRIPTURE WHEEL

Scripture Bouquet Step:

Forget-Me-Nots

Memory Strategy:

Lumping

Supplies:

* crayons or wipe-off markers
* poster board
* clear, self-adhesive contact paper
* scissors
* paper fastener
* copy of the Scripture Wheel

Verse: Any verse you choose to learn or review

Overview: What's more captivating to kids than a rousing game of Hide 'n Seek? In this fun-to-make activity, kids hide portions of a verse then recall which words are hidden.

The Activity

Photocopy or trace the patterns for the cover-up wheel and wedges on poster board or stiff paper. Invite children to color the patterns for the wheel and the wedges with markers or crayons, then cut out the patterns.

Cover the wheels with clear self-adhesive contact paper or laminate them. Attach the wedges (overlapping their points slightly) to the center of each wheel with a paper fastener.

Use a crayon or wipe-off marker to write any Scripture verse around the edge of each wheel. (Be sure to include the Scripture reference for older kids.) Use the wedges to hide portions of the verse and encourage children to repeat the verse and tell what words are missing. Then switch turns and invite children to quiz you! Erase the verse with a tissue to reuse the Scripture wheel over and over for different verses and reviews.

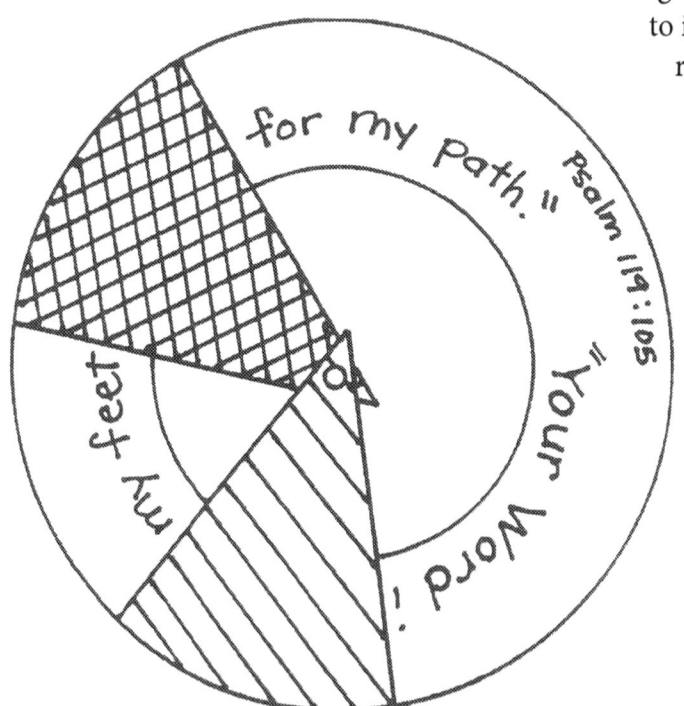

✓ TERIFFIC TIP

Kids enjoy using the Scripture Wheel for review and reinforcement with partners. Have kids choose verses to review in pairs or trios often!

76

Scripture Wheel Pattern

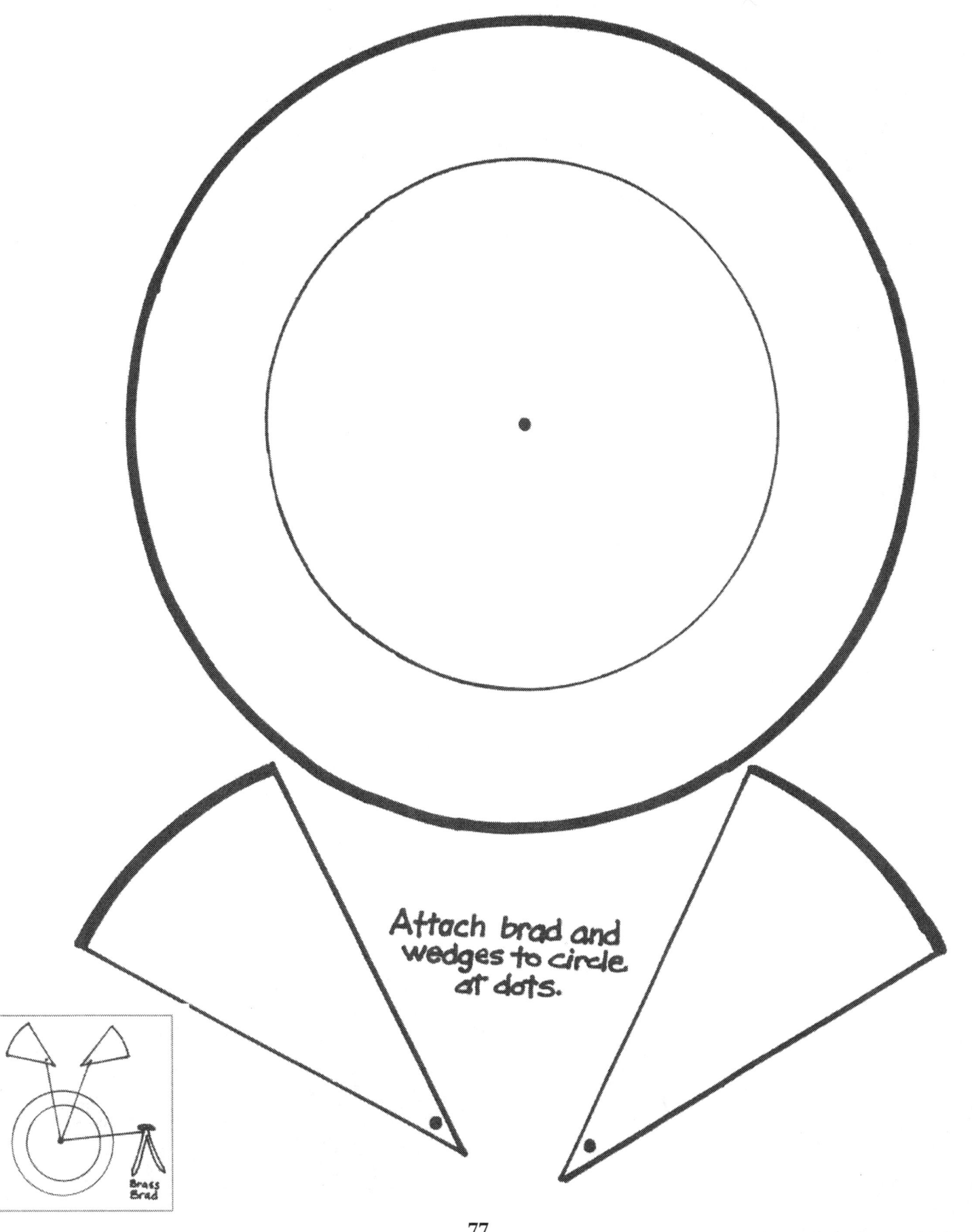

USE YOUR NOODLE!

Scripture Bouquet Step:

Tulips

Memory Strategy:

Lettering;
Manipulatives

✂

Supplies:

✽ uncooked alphabet noodles

✽ a shallow bowl

✽ paper plates

✽ markers

✽ crackers

Verse: Any verse you choose to learn or reinforce

Overview: Invite your child to turn into a "souper" chef and use alphabet soup noodles to recreate the verse you're learning. And don't miss the next creative craft activity which also helps kids use their "noodles!"

The Activity

Place crackers (one per child) on a paper plate in the center of a table. Fill a shallow bowl with uncooked alphabet noodles and set the bowl in the center of the table beside the crackers.

Distribute the paper plates and have children write the Scripture verse you're learning or reviewing on their plates. Hand each person a small pile of noodles from the bowl.

On "go," everyone races to recreates the Scripture verse by placing noodle letters on top of the written letters on their plates. If someone is missing a needed letter, her or she can ask another player if for that letter or go "fishing" in the soup bowl for the letter. As soon as a player completes the verse, have that person munch down a cracker and whistle—then repeat the verse aloud.

FOOD FOR THE SOUL

Make a pot of Veggie-Verse Soup! Pour alphabet noodles in a pot of broth and add cooked vegetables. Remind kids that we become healthy when we feed our bodies with healthy food and our lives with God's nutritious Word!

78

CARD BATTLE

Verse: Any verse you choose to learn or review

Overview: Exciting, action-games are a great way to overcome what often turns into tedious repetition. Whether played in pairs at home or in groups at church, Card Battle is sure to become a favorite way to review verses.

The Activity

Choose one to six verses to play the game. Have kids write lumped portions of each verse on separate index cards so that when they're finished writing, there are complete verses for review. (Be sure to include a reference card for each verse.) It may be helpful to write each verse and reference on a 3 x 5 card and lay the card on the table for players to refer to as they play.

Shuffle and divide the cards to among the players. (It's fine if one player has an extra card.) Take turns choosing cards from each other's hands and collecting lumped phrases or words to reconstruct the review verses.

When a player has made a completed verse, he or she may lay it on the table in its correct order, then repeat the verse and Scripture reference aloud. The player with the most completed verses is the winner.

> For a challenging variation, lay the cards face down in rows of five. Take turns turning over cards. If the two cards turned over are "neighboring lumps" of the same verse, lay them face up in front of you. Continue until you've reconstructed the entire verse.

Scripture Bouquet Step: Forget-Me-Nots

Memory Strategy: Lumping

Supplies:
* index cards
* markers

HIDDEN IN YOUR

Scripture Bouquet Step:
Roses; Forget-Me-Nots

Memory Strategy:
Lumping; Visualizing

Supplies:
* red cardstock, poster board, or construction paper
* markers
* scissors & glue
* slips of paper
* heart pattern on facing page
* hole punch (optional)

Verse: Any verses you choose to review and reinforce

Overview: Use a cheery poster board heart as a manipulative and let children reconstruct a Scripture verse while they answer questions.

The Activity

Before this activity, photocopy or trace the heart pattern from the opposite page on sturdy, red paper (such as card stock, poster board, or construction paper). Have children cut out the paper hearts, then use a pencil or hole punch to poke seven holes in the paper heart. Invite children to decorate the hearts using markers.

Have each person write the following on slips of paper:

➤ *three slips of paper with lumped portions of a verse*
➤ *three slips with questions concerning the verse's meaning*
➤ *one slip with the Scripture reference written on it*

Direct children to roll the slips of paper into thin scrolls and insert each scroll through a hole in the paper hearts. Have children form pairs or trios and take turns drawing out the scrolls to reconstruct the verse and reference and answer the questions. Or invite each person to "share his heart" and have the whole class answer the questions and reconstruct the verses!

TRY THIS! This is a wonderful activity for reviewing previously learned verses. Write three verses on paper, their references on three other slip, and draw a small heart on one slip. Insert the scolls into the holes, then take turns choosing scrolls to match up verses with references. If the heart is drawn, that player must recite any verse he or she knows.

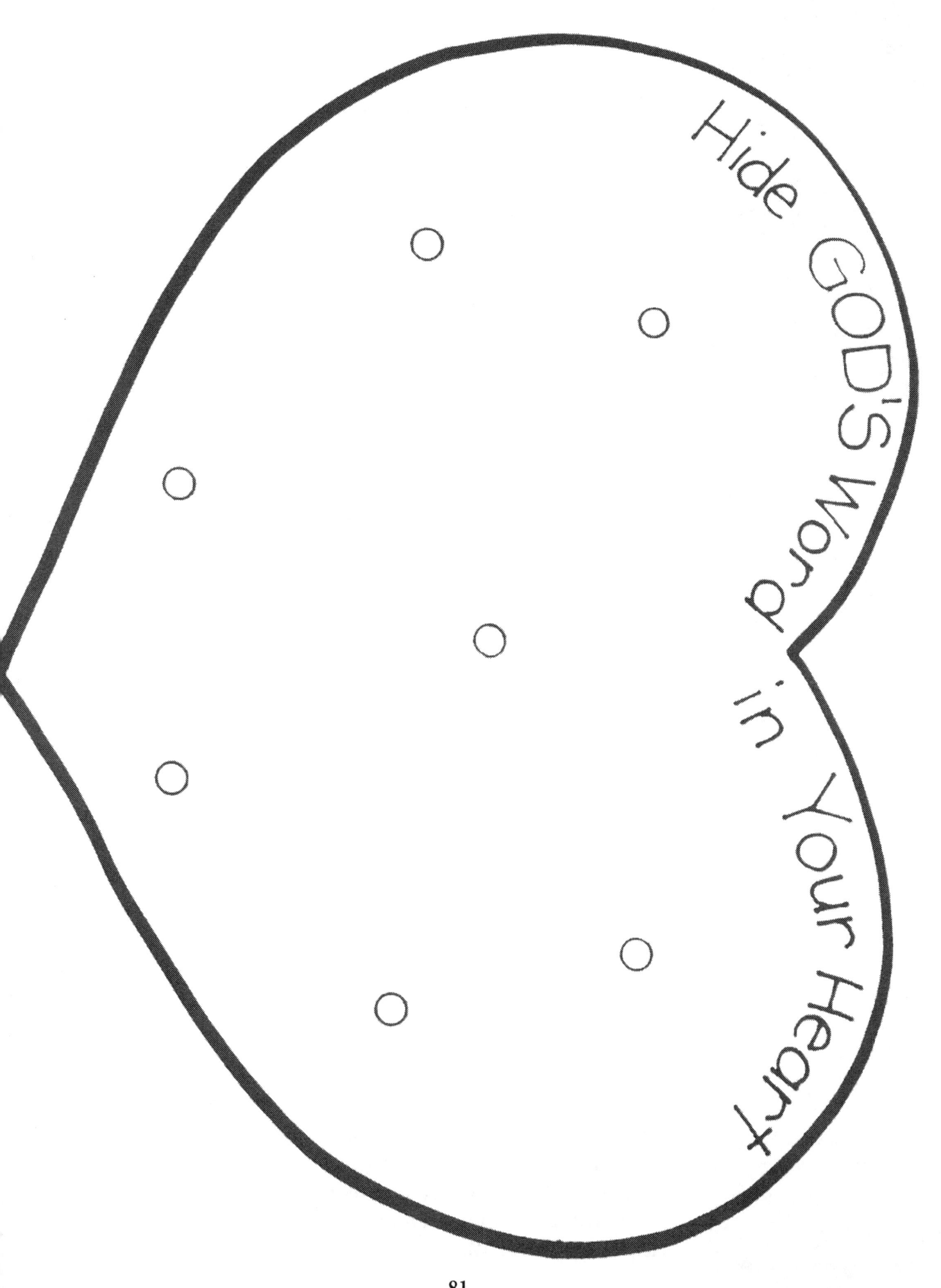

DAZED & A-MAZED

Scripture Bouquet Step:

Tulips;
Forget-Me-Nots

Memory Strategy:

Lumping;
Word order

Supplies:

* pencils with erasers
* markers
* copies of the mazes on the next two pages

Verse: Any verse you choose to learn or review

Overview: Mazes offer problem solving, cognitive reasoning, and good old-fashioned fun! Utilize their motivational appeal with older children by adding the words to any verse that eventually leads them to the Finish Line. Remind your child that God's Word helps them keep them on the right path every time.

The Activity

Photocopy the maze patterns from the following two pages. Make enough copies so that every child has copies of both puzzles.

Choose a verse to learn or several verses to review. Distribute pencils, then direct children to solve one of the maze patterns using the pencil erasers as "lines" along the puzzle. When they discover the correct path, have children write the words to a verse along that path from Start to Finish. Now add words at random along the rest of the pathways.

Have children exchange papers to solve the verse hen write the completed verse along the bot- he pages. Older kids will enjoy having blank sheets of paper to make their own puzzle designs and add verses to be solved. Photocopy the puzzles then place them in a large paper sack. Invite kids to each choose a puzzle to solve—then have the person who invented the puzzle check it.

Invite kids to use crayons and markers to decorate the mazes after solving them. Hang the completed puzzles on a wall with the caption: *God's Word Helps Us Find Our Way!*

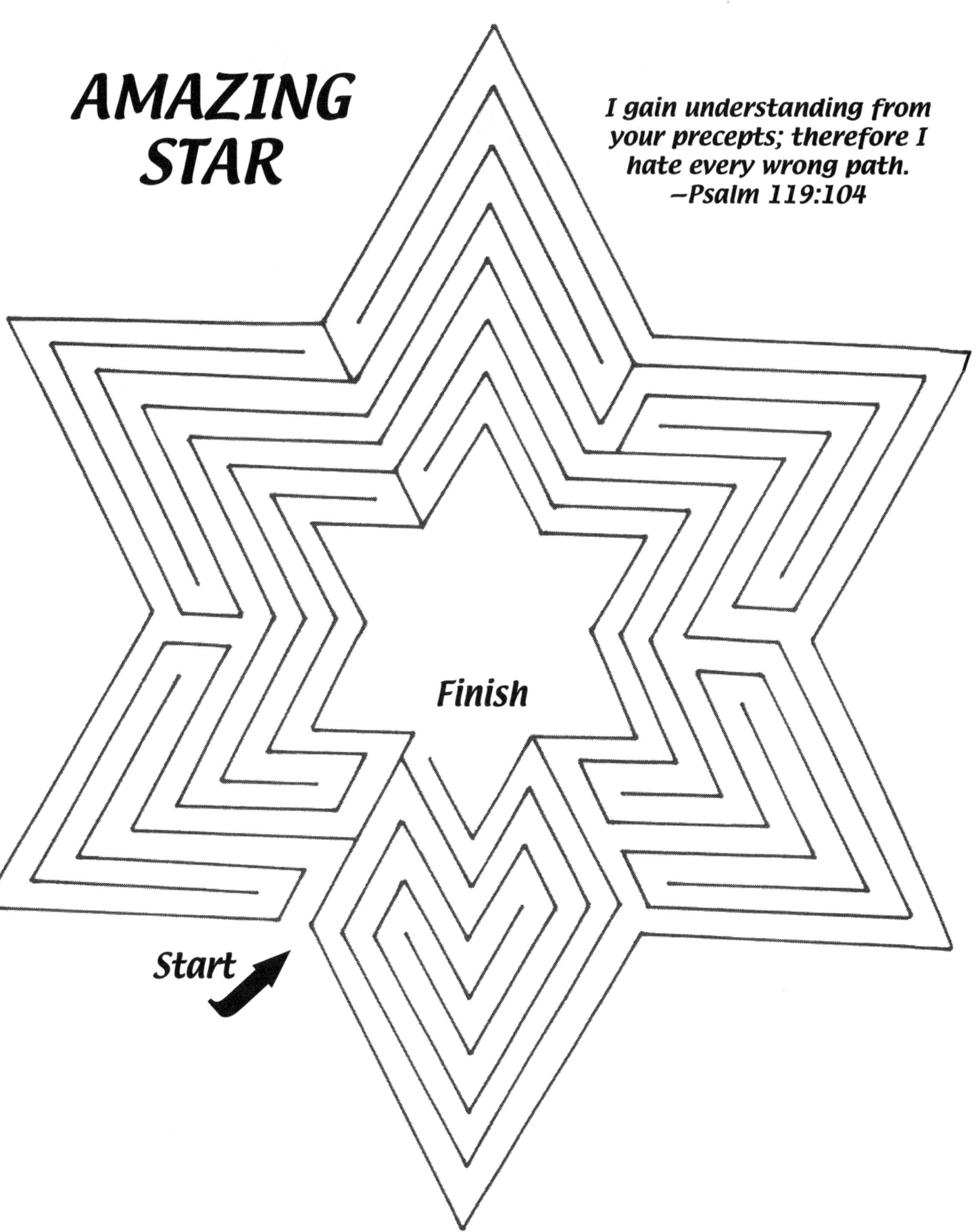

THE HIDDEN WORD

I have hidden your word in my heart that I might not sin against you.
—Psalm 119:11

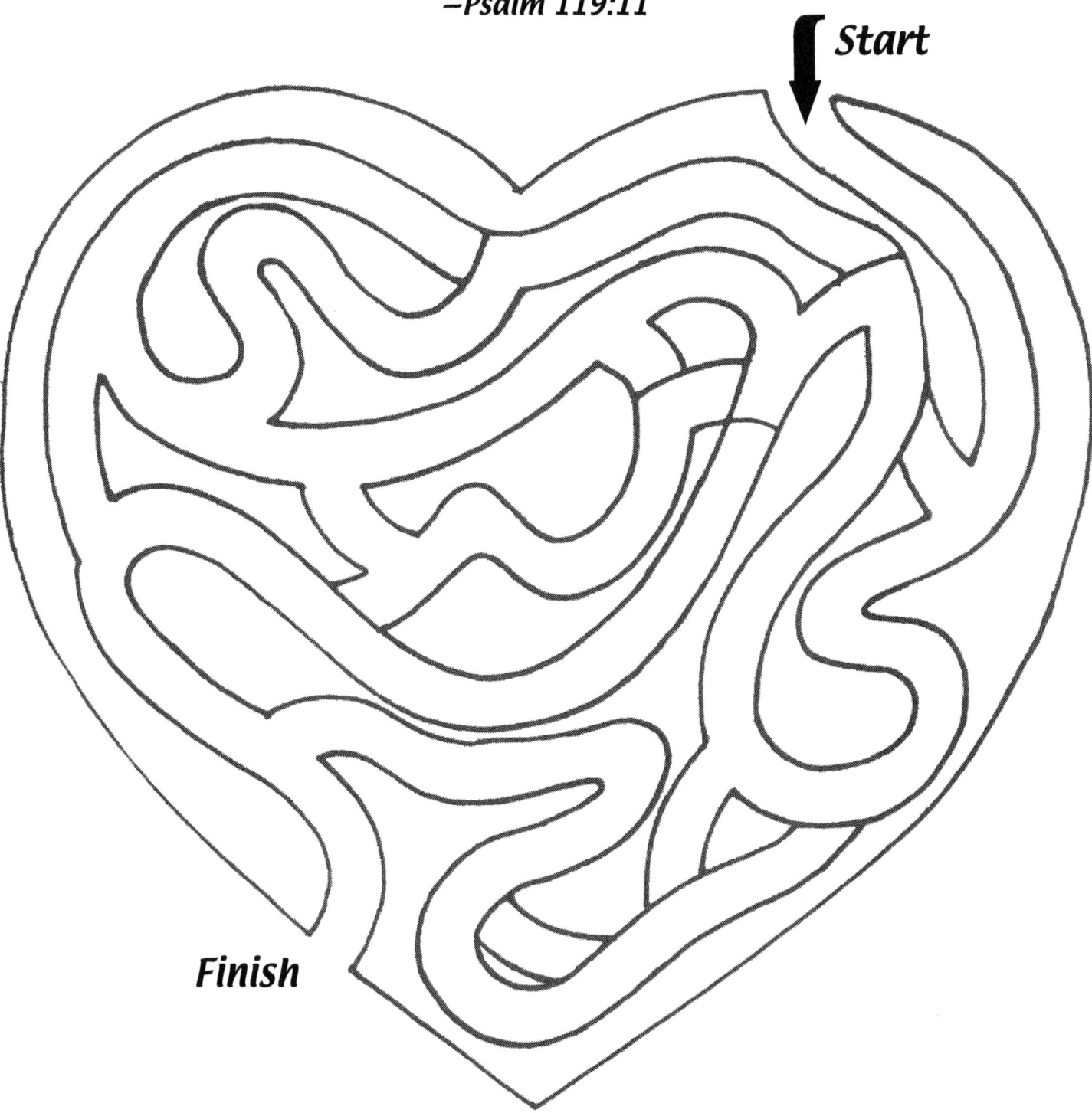

STICKER DOODLES

Verse: Any verse you want to reinforce or enrich

Overview: Offer older kids the joy of creating a Scripture plate to remind them of the importance "serving up" God's Word.

The Activity

Distribute plastic plates and set the other craft items on a table. Have kids choose various letter stickers to "write" the verse you're reviewing in the center of the plates. Challenge kids to lump the phrases in the verse and stick the words in separate lines if possible. As they works, ask questions such as, *"What does this verse say to you?" "How can this verse help you this week?"* and *"Why do you think God wanted us to know what this verse says?"*

When the letters to the Scripture verse are in place, invite kids to read the verses aloud. Let kids rev up their creative juices and decorate the rims of the plates using feathers and colorful paint pens.

When the plates are dry, encourage kids to use them to serve others (dry foods such as bread, crackers, or cookies). Remind kids that learning Scripture is the perfect way to serve God, too! Challenge kids to read the verse on their plate every day for two weeks until it's memorized.

Older children are just as "crafty" as younger kids—they love making handy crafts to use at home. Combine Scripture and crafts whenever possible to make memory work truly *memorable!*

Scripture Bouquet Step:

Roses;
Forget-Me-Nots

Memory Strategy:

Visualizing;
Manipulatives;
Lumping

Supplies:

* 6-inch plastic plates
* craft glue
* a variety of self-adhesive alphabet stickers
* paint pens
* tape
* craft feathers

TIC-TAC-WOW!

Verse: Any verses you choose to learn or review

Overview: Repetition is key for committing something to long-term memory. Make repetition fun and motivating with an old favorite—Tic-Tac-Toe.

The Activity

Before playing, cut a sheet of blue craft foam lengthwise into four 1-inch wide strips. Cut five triangle shapes from a sheet of yellow craft foam and five circle or square shapes from a sheet of red craft foam. Make a set of strips, circles and triangles for every two players.

Have kids write the verse you're learning or reviewing on index cards. Demonstrate how to lay the craft foam strips on the floor or on a table in a traditional Tic-Tac-Toe game board pattern. Place the Scripture cards face down. Have partners or teams of players choose either the triangles or the circles. Take turns repeating the Scripture verse (only one peek at a card is allowed during a game). Each time the verse is correctly repeated, place a shape on the game board. Continue until someone places three shapes in a row across, down, or diagonally. If there's a tie, go for an exciting tie-breaker using review verses!

Store the game in a 10- by 13-inch envelope. Making sturdy games and storing them for easy access provides for quick memory games for years to come!

Scripture Bouquet Step:

Tulips

Memory Strategy:

Manipulatives; Games

Supplies:

* sheets of blue, red, and yellow craft foam
* scissors
* index cards
* markers
* 10- by 13-inch envelopes (optional)

BREAK-IT-DOWN

Verse: Any verse you're learning

Overview: Allowing children to individually decide *how* and *where* to break a verse into manageable pieces will make memorization more effective.

The Activity

Have children cut 24-inch strips of crepe paper. Have each person cut three strips, each a different color. Choose a verse, then have kids print the verse in large letters down the length of each strip (in one long line including the reference). Encourage kids to break the verse into logical, natural breaks.

"We all like sheep have gone astray." Isaiah 53:6

Have kids read the verse a few times aloud, then challenge them to decide where they would break the verse into smaller parts. Have kids tear the verse into segments (or lumps). Repeat the same procedure for each long verse strip, breaking the verse in the same way each time. Remind kids that not everyone will necessarily break his or her verse in just the same way. (Isaiah 53:6 has been cut apart in several ways below as an example.)

When the tears are made, have kids tape the pieces of their verse portions back in order but mixing up the colors. Kids should each have three long verse strips in interesting colors to hang up at home for review.

For an extra challenge with older children, scramble the pieces face-down, then take turns turning over the pieces and fitting them together. Read each piece as it's turned over.

Scripture Bouquet Step:

Tulips;

Memory Strategy:

Lumping;
Visualizing

Supplies:

* markers
* scissors
* rolls of crepe paper (several colors)
* clear tape

SWORD OF THE SPIRIT

Scripture Bouquet Step:

Roses;
Forget-Me-Nots

Memory Strategy:

Games;
Manipulatives

Supplies:

* poster board
* scissors
* markers
* paper fasteners
* pretzel sticks (optional)
* juice & cups (optional)

Verse: Any verse you choose to review

Overview: This is a great game for reviewing several verses you've already learned.

The Activity

Photocopy the game board patterns from the facing page then glue them to a sheet of poster board. Color the patterns (game board, spinner, and arrows) with bright markers. Cut out the patterns and attach the two arrows to the center of each wheel using paper fasteners (the larger arrow on the game board and the small arrow on the spinner wheel). You may wish to poke holes through the patterns prior to adding the paper fasteners as this will allow the arrows to spin more freely.

Tack the game board to a bulletin board or lay it on a table or the floor. Review the verse you're reinforcing aloud several times. Then take turns spinning the number wheel. The player or team with the largest number spins the large wheel. Use the following directions depending on your spin:

- **If you spin a SWORD**—Opponents give a review verse reference to look up in the Bible. Look up the verse, then repeat or read the verse aloud. Score 1 point.

- **If you spin a QUESTION MARK**—opponents (or leader) ask a question concerning one of the review verses. If your answer is correct, score 1 point.

Continue playing until a player or team reaches seven points. Be sure to give each other a pat on the back for a great time and for helping each other learn God's Word!

For extra fun, finish your review time by serving pretzel "swords" and fruit juice.

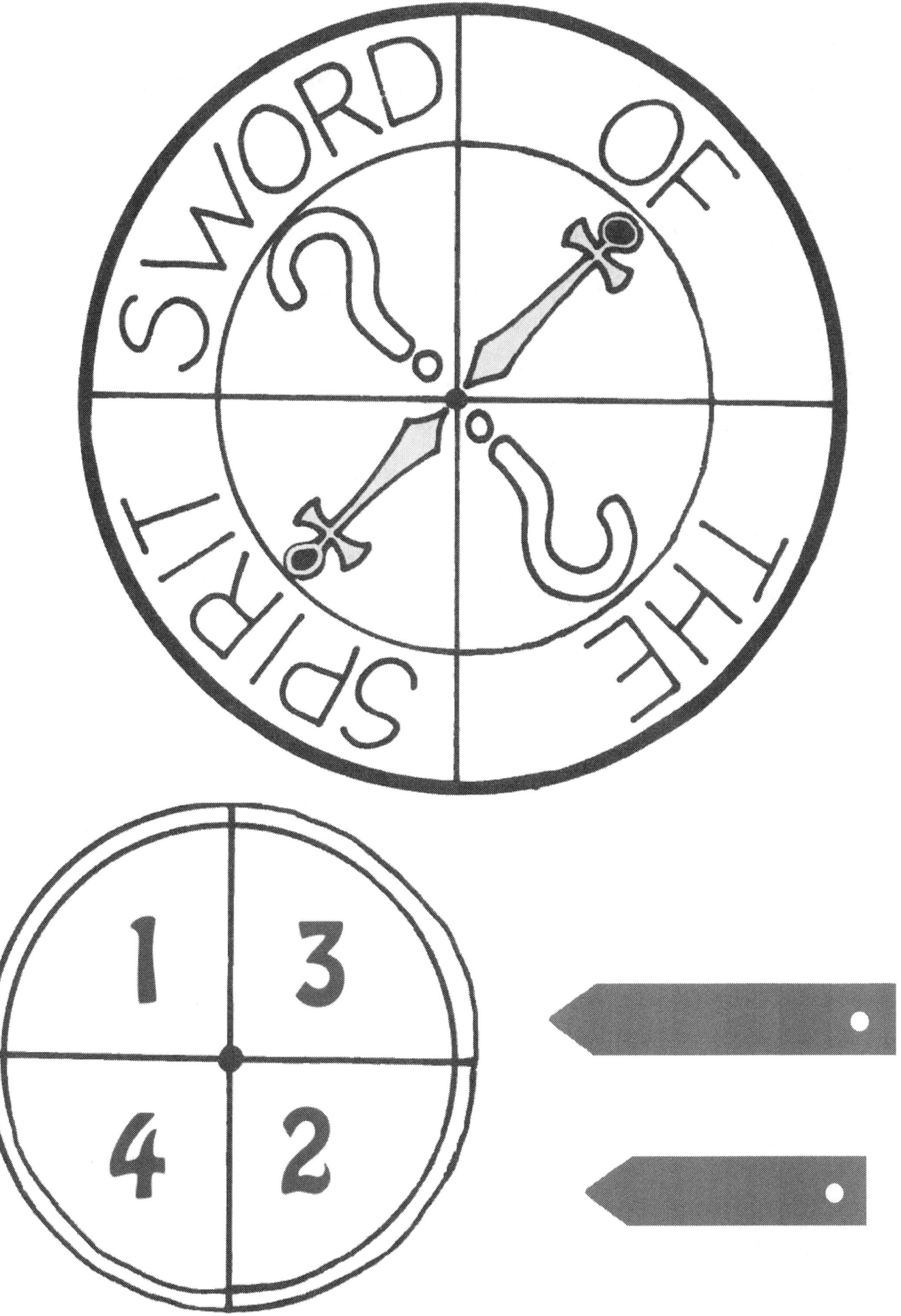

RELAY THE WORD!

Verse: Any verse you choose to review or reinforce

Overview: Kids love balloons! Use this noisy—but lively—relay to review memory verses.

The Activity

Hand each person a balloon, slip of paper, and a marker or pen. Have kids write one of their favorite memory verses and the reference on the slips of paper. Encourage kids to use their Bibles to look up the verses if necessary or use a class list of verses you've worked to learn.

When the verses are written, show kids how to roll their papers like thin scrolls. Then direct kids to insert the paper scrolls into the open end of the balloons. With the slips of paper inside, inflate the balloons and tie the ends in knots. Place all of the balloons at one end of the room and have kids stand at the opposite end. On a "go" signal, have kids hop across the room to choose a balloon to sit on and pop. When the verse is retrieved, have kids hop back to their starting places.

When everyone has a verse, let them read aloud the first couple of words and choose someone to finish repeating the verse. Then briefly review what each verse teaches us and why it's an important verse to remember. Continue until everyone has had a turn to read a verse.

Let kids each make a second Scripture Balloon with hidden verse. Add strands of curled ribbons to make the balloons even more festive. Encourage kids to share the fun—and God's Word—with their families.

Scripture Bouquet Step:

Tulips; Roses; Forget-Me-Nots

Memory Strategy:

Manipulatives; Games

Supplies:

* at least 2 large balloons for each child (not inflated)
* slips of paper
* markers
* scissors
* curling ribbon

SCRIPTURE SCRAMBLER

Verse: Any verse you choose to review

Overview: Kids love the challenge of puzzles and of unscrambling words. In addition, writing words to verses makes a concrete connection between the abstract and the physical.

The Activity

Using the illustration as a model, choose a verse to scramble. In the Word Bank, list the correct words to the verse, but do not list them in order. Repeat the preparation steps for another review verse on the flip side of the poster board.

Distribute paper and pens or pencils. Challenge kids to see if they can unscramble the review verse by using all of the words, in their correct order, from the Word Bank. Allow kids to work the puzzle in pairs or trios.

When one side of the Scripture Scrambler is finished, point out any patterns or lists in the verse. Then turn the poster board around and challenge kids to see if they can solve another scrambled verse.

Kids enjoy making their own scrambled verses for friends to solve. Hand each person a sheet of paper and have everyone scramble a verse and add a Word Bank. Photocopy the pages and staple them into a book with construction paper covers that kids decorate then take home to complete.

Scripture Bouquet Step:

Forget-Me-Nots

Memory Strategy:

Lettering; Patterning

Supplies:

* paper
* pens or pencils
* poster board
* tape

Word Bank

anyone	his
love	truly
But	made
God's	him
obeys	if
complete	is
1 John	in
word	2:5

complete God's if anyone But truly obeys made his word, John love is in

— 2:5 him 1

SHEMA OLYMPICS

Scripture Bouquet Step:
Roses

Memory Strategy:
Visualization; Listing; Patterning

Supplies:
* poster board
* markers
* a bag of large marshmallows
* tape
* photocopies of the events card
* scissors
* 1-inch wide blue ribbon

Verse: "Love the Lord your God with all your heart and with all your soul and with all your mind and with all your strength" Mark 12:30.

Overview: Give kids memorable fun to help them learn this all-important verse about loving God.

The Activity

Before you begin the Shema Olympics, write Mark 12:30 on a sheet of poster board. Write the words in black except for the following and their appropriate colors: "heart" (red), "soul" (yellow), "mind" (blue), "strength" (purple). Draw a heart around the word "Love." These color and shape embellishments will help kids make visual tie-ins to the list of *how* we're to love God. Tape the poster board where everyone can read it. Photocopy the events card (from the opposite page), one per person.

> Tell kids that the Shema was an ancient, Hebrew praise to worship our one God. It was repeated twice daily—at morning and evening prayers.

Have kids repeat the verse two time. Then point out the color-coded words and the heart shape. Point out that the word "heart" comes first in A-B-C order and that beginning "S" words (soul and strength) alternate with "heart" and "mind." If kids have trouble recalling which "S" word comes first, point out that in A-B-C order, the "so-" in soul comes before the "st-" in strength. Instruct kids to look at the verse for a few seconds, then close their eyes and picture the word order of the four words in the list (heart, soul, mind, strength). Then repeat the verse three times aloud.

Briefly discuss what this verse teaches us about the ways we're to love God. Ask kids to tell how each word in the list helps us love God more completely and powerfully. Then hand each person a large marshmallow and an events card. Break into teams or partners and challenge them to complete all four events in the Shema Olympics.

After everyone finishes their Olympic events, have teams or partners share their insights from the questions as they nibble their marshmallows. Explain to kids that even something as simple as marshmallow have a purpose—and that something as important as God's Word has life-changing purposes and power! Tell kids to remember the sweetness of God's Word every time they eat a marshmallow. Then present a blue ribbon to each person who can repeat the Shema (Mark 12:30).

SHEMA OLYMPICS
Events Card

Using a large marshmallow, complete the following event with your team members or partner. As you complete and compete, think about how these events relate to the Shema which teaches us to: *"Love the Lord your God with all your heart and with all your soul and with all your mind and with all your strength"* Mark 12:30.

Event #1: The Heart. Hold the marshmallow to your heart and tell one reason why the marshmallow is lovable.

Event #2: The Soul. Describe the inside of the marshamallow without breaking it apart.

Event #3. The Mind. Think of 3 uses for a marshmallow.

Event #4: The Strength. Squash the marshmallow with all your might, then puff it up again.

- How do the heart, soul, mind, and strength help us love God?
- Could we love God as well if one was missing? Why not?
- How can you love God more this week?

Scripture Bouquet Step:

Roses;
Forget-Me-Nots

Memory Strategy:

Games;
Manipulatives

Supplies:

* cardstock & index cards
* markers
* scissors
* colored cereal loops
* a penny
* copy of the gameboard on facing page
* copy of the game cards

HIDDEN IN HEART

Verse: Any series of review verses

Overview: Board games offer a quiet, relaxed way to reinforce verse memorization and increase understanding.

The Activity

Photocopy the game board and game cards onto sturdy card stock. Cut apart the game cards. Color the game boards. Write at least five review verses on index cards, one verse per card.

Choose if you'll use one review verse at a time or if each person will use a different review verse (hand out the index cards if each person is to have a verse). Shuffle the game cards and lay them on the game board. Have each player choose a different color of cereal loop (for a marker) and place the loops at "Start."

Take turns flipping a penny to see how many spaces you'll move. *Heads* moves you ahead two spaces and *tails* moves you one space. Follow any directions on the spaces on which you land. If a player lands on a space with **lips**, repeat the review verse. If a player lands on a space with a **question mark**, a card is drawn from the pile and must be answered. Continue until all players reach the center of the heart.

What are the FIRST and LAST words in the verse?	Give the REFERENCE for the verse.	What does this verse MEAN?
In which book of the BIBLE is this verse found?	How can you put this verse into ACTION in your life?	Why is this an IMPORTANT verse to know, understand, and use?

94

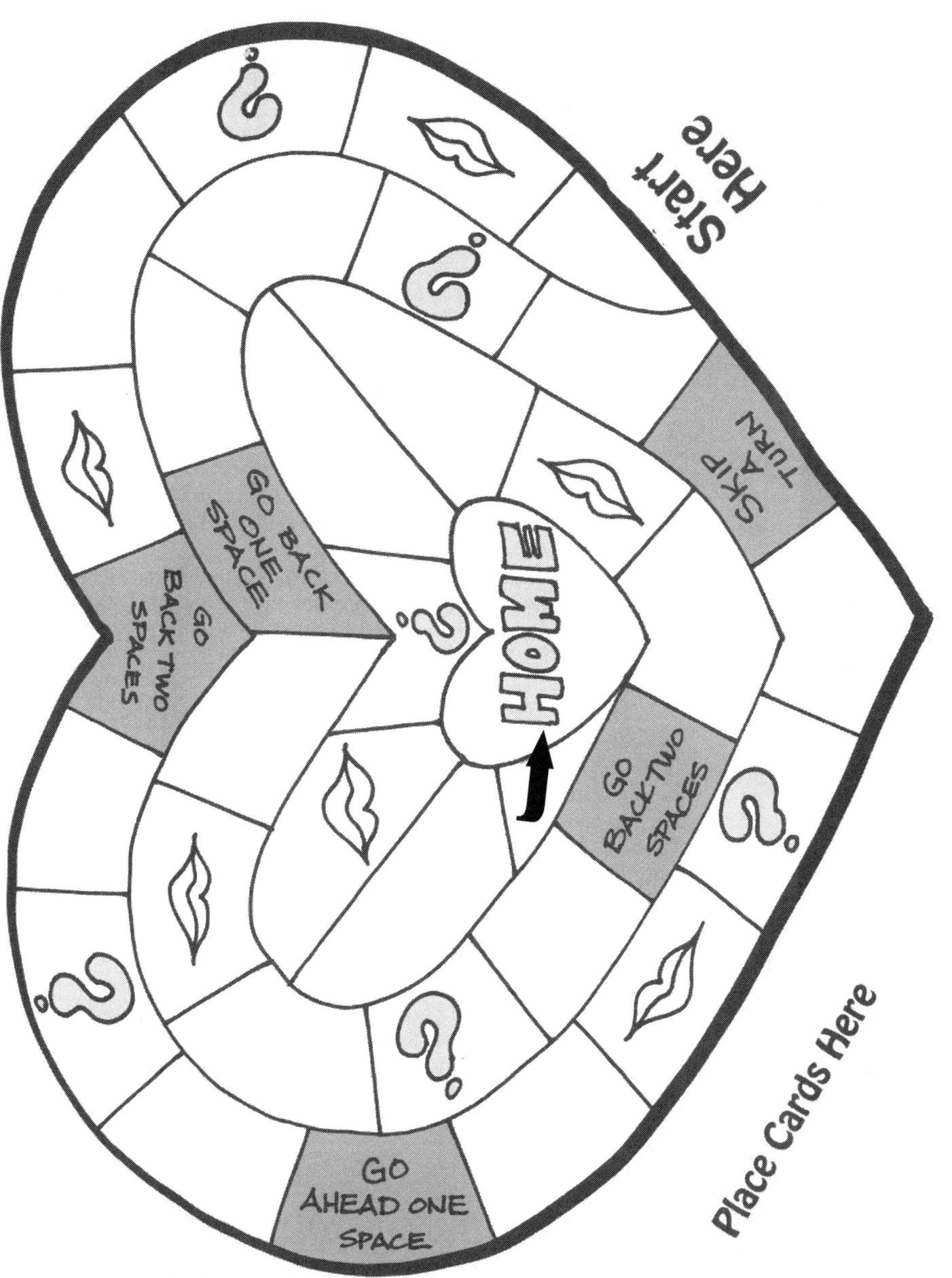

BUILD-A-VERSE

Scripture Bouquet Step:

Tulips

Memory Strategy:

Lumping; Games

Supplies:

* construction paper or poster board
* index cards
* markers
* two rolls of tape

Verse: Any verse you choose to learn or review

Overview: Use this relay to help kids physically see portions of a verse, then reconstruct the verse in correct word order.

The Activity

Cut two 10-inch heart shapes from construction paper or poster board. Cut index cards in half lengthwise. Write lumped portions of the verse you're learning or reviewing on each card. Prepare two identical sets of cards. Tape the hearts to a wall or door and about a foot apart.

Form two teams and have them stand in lines at the opposite end of the room from the hearts. Place a set of verse cards on the floor at the head of each line. Hand tape to one player on each team and position those players next to the hearts. The are the Tapers.

On "go," the first player from each team runs to his or her team's paper heart and positions the verse portion on the heart shape. The Taper tapes the card in place, then hands the tape to the teammate who brought the card, who then becomes the next Taper. (The last Taper returns to the back of his or her team's line.)

Continue adding cards to the verses. (You may need to adjust cards already in place!) Play until one team has correctly reconstructed the Scripture verse. Encourage players to help each other if they're stuck on word order.

 **Remember:** Action-packed relays are always fun, but be sure to cool down with short discussions of how the verse you're learning can help during the coming week!

THE GREAT COVER-UP

Verse: Any verse you choose to learn or review

Overview: Kids take turns covering up words to a verse, then challenge friends to recite it—missing words and all!

The Activity

On a sheet of poster board, write the words to a verse you're learning or one you're reviewing. Space the words a bit far apart and lines apart wide enough to tape cards over words to hide them. Tape the poster board to a wall so kids can read it. You'll need to keep a small stack of index cards and a roll of tape handy as you play.

Seat everyone in a circle and hand one child an index card. Explain to kids that they'll pass the card around the circle until you say, "Cover up!" Whoever is holding the index card will go to the verse and choose a word to cover up using the index card and tape. Then that child can call on someone to repeat the verse with the missing word. If correct, the card stays in place. If the verse is not repeated correctly, the index card is passed around the circle again.

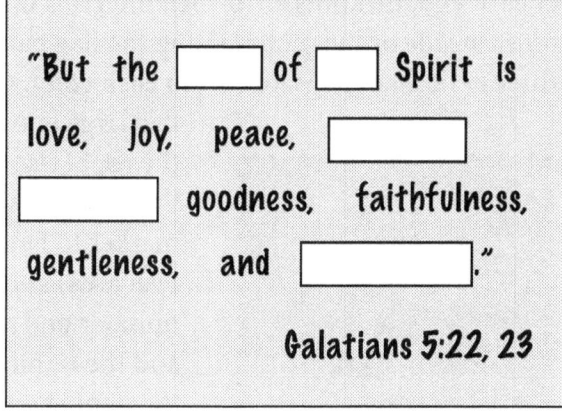

Continue playing until all of the words to the verse are hidden by index cards and a player correctly repeats the verse. Play again uncovering the words this time!

Even hard-to-motivate older kids like word games when you combine action, strategy, and lots of laughter!

Scripture Bouquet Step:

Tulips;
Forget-Me-Nots

Memory Strategy:

Lumping;
Lettering;
Games

Supplies:

* poster board
* markers
* index cards
* tape

Scripture Bouquet Step:

Tulips;
Forget-Me-Nots

Memory Strategy:

Games;
Manipulatives

Supplies:

* jute or rope (about 1/2-inch thick)
* scissors
* craft foam sheets (green, blue, white)
* permanent markers
* twist-tie wire

TUG-O-WAR

Verse: Any verse you choose to learn or reinforce

Overview: Constant back-and-forth repetition makes this a great game to play when initially learning a shorter verse. Play Tug-O-War with partners or entire teams.

The Activity

Before playing, cut a 6-foot length of sturdy jute (thick enough to withhold tugging at both ends). Tie a knot in the center of the rope. Beginning at each end, tie knots at 10-inch intervals until there are six to eight knots on each side of the center. Using the flag pattern on the facing page, cut three craft foam flags, one from each color. Cut a hole in the corner of each flag large enough to slide over the knots in the rope. Use a twist-tie wire to attach the white flag to the center knot. Use a permanent marker to label one flag number one (in the oval area) and the other number two. Slide the number one flag onto the first knot at one end and the number two flag onto the first knot at the opposite end.

Have two (teams or partners) each hold an end of the rope. Take turns reciting the Scripture verse and reference you're learning or reviewing. Each time one side correctly repeats the verse, they can move their flag one knot closer to the center. The team reaching the center knot first is the winning team. (If your class is very large, consider making several Tug-O-War ropes and flag sets.)

TRY THIS! After a few tug-o-war matches, serve rope licorice as a special treat! Or try playing the game with an edible licorice rope. Tie knots in your rope and each time you repeat the verse, nibble a knot!

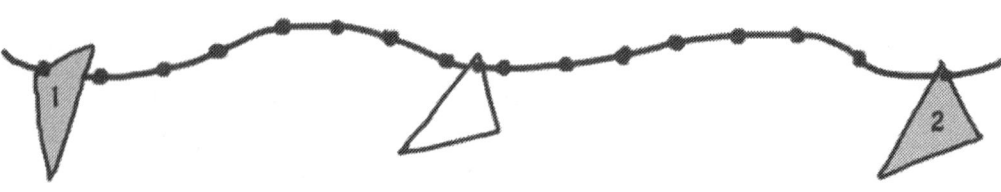

Tug-O-War Flag Pattern

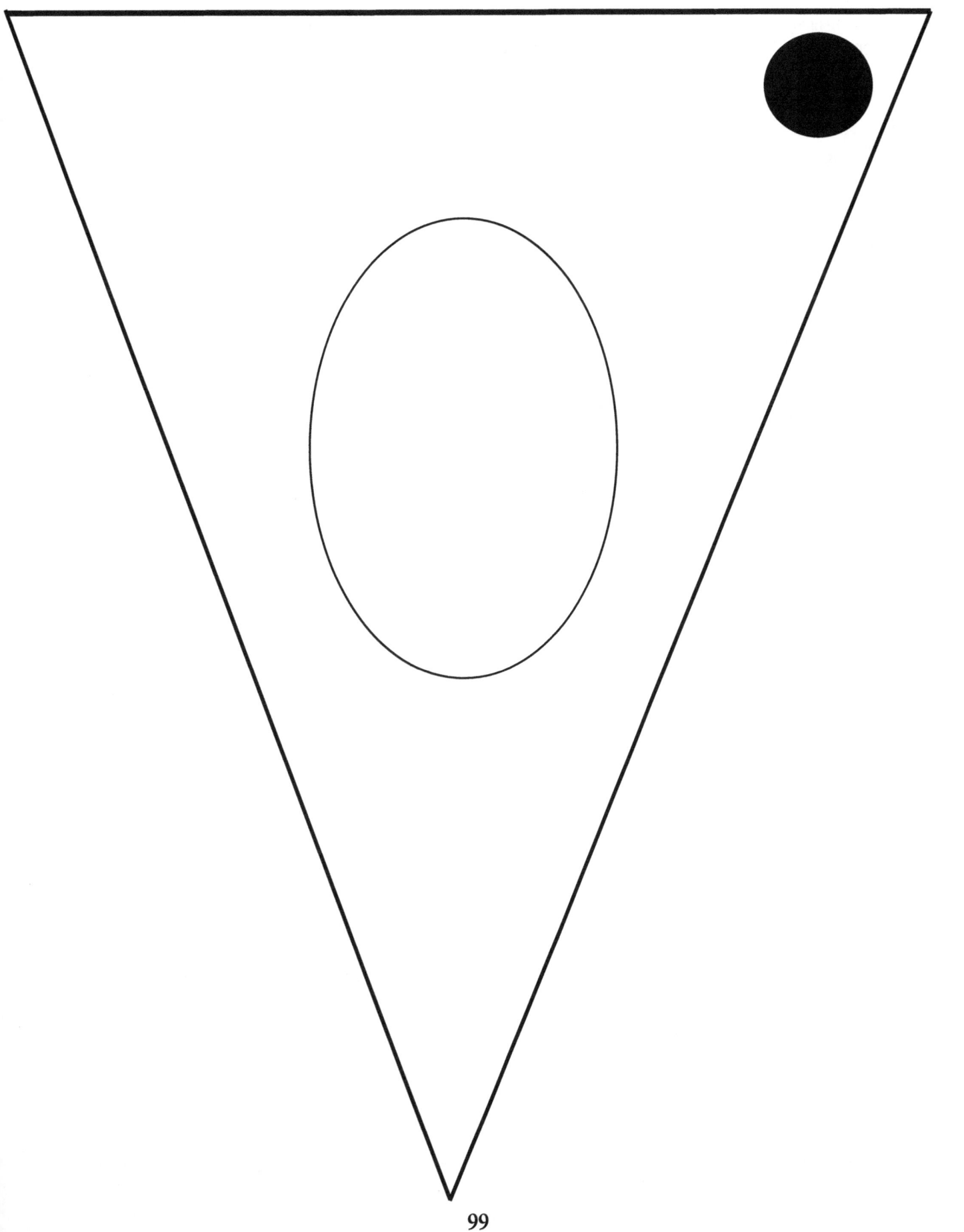

LEARNING SCRIPTURE IS A BLAST!

Photocopy this page. Write the verse you're memorizing next to the rocket. Each time you practice the verse, color a shape on the page. When you're finished with this outta sight picture, save it in a special folder for review!

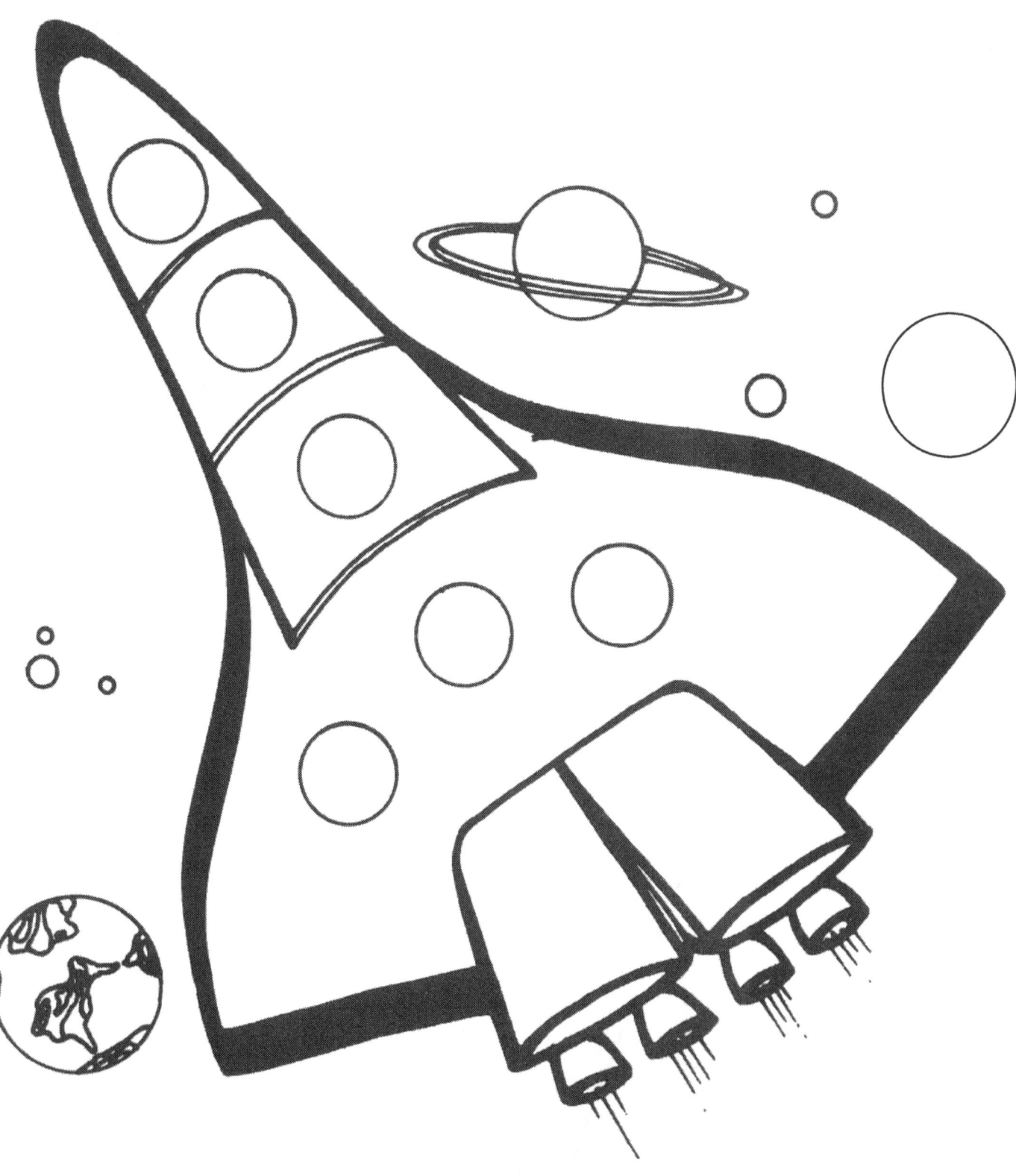

Permission to photocopy for church, school, or home use only. Taken from *Scripture Memory Makers*
© Susan Lingo, Susan Lingo Books, 2007.

SCRIPTURE IS BELL-RINGIN' FUN!

Photocopy this page. Write the verse you're memorizing above the pinball bumpers. Each time you practice the verse, color a shape on the page. When you're finished, save the page in a special folder for review!

Permission to photocopy for church, school, or home use only. Taken from *Scripture Memory Makers*
© Susan Lingo, Susan Lingo Books, 2007.

BASIC BIBLE SKILLS

A natural to go along with learning to recall, understand, and apply Scripture is learning about the Bible and developing the skills needed to use and study God's Word for a lifetime. Knowing the basics of how the Bible is set up, organized, and utilized will help children in every stage of Scripture memorization and application. But just as God's Word must be presented in age-appropriate ways for various ages, Bible skills must also reflect a child's age, developmental stage, and most importantly, his or her reading ability. Children in preschool can learn that the Bible is God's Word and is always true and good. But a third grade class will go well beyond these simple, but powerful truths. These older, more literate, kids are ready for naming books of the Bible in order, locating specific verses throughout the Old and New Testaments, and beginning to use the concordance and simple Bible commentaries. Here are three categories of basic skills children can begin to learn along with memorizing and learning to apply God's Word—the first step in Bible literacy:

▶ *How the Bible Is Physically Organized*

▶ *Key Events, People, & Places*

▶ *Bible-Study and Reference Tools*

On the facing page, you'll discover a chart with numerous, basic skills goals for children in three age levels. These basic skills form the foundation of an effective course of study for tools that will enable children to develop and hone Bible-study skills to last their entire lives. And on page 104-105, there are quick ideas to get you started! Knowing Scripture and how to apply it starts kids on the path toward God's will and power—knowing how to use the Bible, through studying God's Word, will strengthen their faith every day. Begin to *use* the Word—begin to *learn* the Book!

More great resources for teaching kids about the Bible and God's Word!

- *Basic Bible Skills*
  (Susan L. Lingo, Standard Publishing)
- *Making Scripture Memorable*
  (Susan L. Lingo, Susan Lingo Books)

Basic Bible Skills Goals by Age Level

3-6 YEAR OLDS	7-9 YEAR OLDS	10-12 YEAR OLDS
• Know that the Bible is God's Word. • Understand that God gave us the Bible. • Learn that God's Word is always true and good for us. • Realize that "Scripture" is another word for God's Word. • Know that the Bible is divided into two main parts: the *Old Testament* and the *New Testament*. • Learn that God wants us to learn, understand, and use His Word. • Know there is help and power in God's Word. • Realize that we treat the Bible with care, respect, and joy.	• Accomplish all goals for 3-6-year-olds. • Learn that the Bible is divided into 66 smaller books. • Know the names of the books of the Bible in order. • Realize that God *inspired* humans to write down His Word. • Understand how to read and write a Bible reference: "book chapter:verse." • Use a beginning *concordance* to find a specific verse. • Use a Bible *dictionary* to look up words in Scripture. • Find OT and NT books and locate specific verses in the Bible. • Understand the differences between the Old and New Testaments. • Name main people, places, and events in correct order in Old and New Testaments.	• Accomplish all goals for 3-9-year-olds. • Identify and name the major divisions in both the Old and New Testaments. • Identify and repeat key phrases and themes in both the Old and New Testaments. • Learn, understand, and be able to apply longer passages and multiple verses. • Use the concordance for word, theme, and other Bible-related studies. • Show evidence of understanding God's Word in deeds and actions—can apply the Word in daily life. • Locate major passages in Scripture including Christ's birth and resurrection, verse on salvation and serving God and others. • Paraphrase meanings and how they relate to our lives and faith.

For the word of the Lord is right and true. —Psalm 33:4

Quick Bible Skill Builders

IDEAS FOR IDENTIFYING BOOKS OF THE BIBLE

Make several sets of book cards for kids to use in learning Bible book names, spelling the titles, ordering the books of the Bible, and identifying major Bible divisions. Make the cards from sturdy paper, index cards, or neon card stock. Use markers to write the names of the books, one title per card. Be sure to make several sets, then use them with these activities:

Book Concentration. Choose whether to use books of the Old or New Testaments, then use two sets of cards for those books. Shuffle the cards and place them face down on the floor or a table. Take turns turning over two cards at a time. If a match is made, draw again. If a match is not made, flip the cards face down and let the next person choose two cards. Play until all the cards have been matched.

Space Race. Choose whether to use books of the Old or New Testaments, then use one set of cards for those books. Divide the cards among players, holding back six or seven cards. Choose a card to place on the floor or set on a chalk rail. The players with the books just before and just after run to place their cards in the spaces in front of and behind the card. The first player to fill the space places a card on the rail for the next turn. Continue until all the cards have been used. (You may wish to allow cards to be used more than once.)

Grab Bag. Use one set of book cards for both the Old and New Testaments. Place the cards in a paper bag. Take turns drawing out cards and telling whether that book is in the Old or New Testament. Older kids can also tell which books come before and after the book title on the card.

Bible Book Burglar. Choose whether to use books of the Old or New Testaments, then use one set of cards for those books. Place a chair in front of the room and have one child sit in the chair facing away from the other kids. Silently flash a book card to the players seated behind the child in the chair, then place the card face down on the floor under the chair. Point to someone to "steal" the book card and hide it in his or her lap. Then have the child sitting in the chair ask questions to try and identify which Bible book card was snatched. If the card isn't identified after six questions, have the child hiding the card become the next person to sit in the chair. If a card is guessed correctly, that child may choose another person to take his or her place in the chair.

About-Face Books. Choose whether to use books of the Old or New Testaments, then use one set of cards for those books. Sit everyone in a circle and begin passing a book card (or two if your group is large). When you say, "About-face!", have kids change passing directions. When you say, "Freeze!" have the player holding the card set in on the floor in the center of the circle. As more cards are added, be sure they're placed in correct order. Continue until all of the cards are in order in the center of the circle. Repeat the order aloud simultaneously.

IDEAS FOR LOCATING SCRIPTURE REFERENCES

Make several sets of number cards to go along with the Bible book cards you've prepared. Using these cards in a variety of fun ways, kids can learn how to locate Scripture references, how to read references, how to tell which numbers come first—the chapter or verse, and many more basic skills. Again, make cards from bright, inviting papers and card stock. Consider inviting kids to design their own cards using a computer and run off color copies on sturdy card stock. Make the cards from sturdy paper, index cards, or neon card stock. Use markers to write numerals on the cards, one numeral per card. Also, prepare several cards with dashes (—) and several with colons (:). Make other cards as indicated in the activities below:

Puzzle Passages. Make several puzzle cards to indicate references of passages you wish for kids to locate and read. (You may want to make puzzles centered around specific themes such as faith, love, or obedience and use verses and passages that deal with the subject.) Cut the book title from the chapter and verse in various cutting patterns (see illustration). Place all of the pieces in a paper sack. Take turns pulling out puzzle pieces and reassembling the puzzles, then locate the passages and read them aloud with brief discussions of what the passages mean.

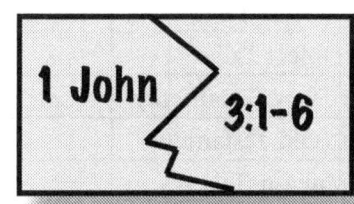

Surprise Book Bags. Label three paper lunch sacks: Book, Chapter, Verse. Place Bible book cards in the Book sack, a handful of number cards in the Chapter sack, and another handful of number cards in the Verse sack. Take turn pulling a card from each sack, first from the Book bag, then the Chapter bag, then the Verse bag. Place the cards together (using the dash and colon cards) to "write out" the Scripture reference. Then locate the verse and read it aloud. If the numbers form a reference for a verse that doesn't exist, replace the cards and draw again. Point out how not all chapters and have the same number of verses and not all books of the Bible have the same number of chapters.

B-C-V Race. You'll need at least five 10-by-4-inch poster board cards, tape, and two sets of colored index-sized cards with the following words on each set (one word per card): "Book," "Chapter," "Verse." (These two sets of cards are the "B-C-V" cards and each team will need a set.) Write Scripture references on the long cards, one reference per card. Form two teams and have them stand at one end of the room. Place one set of B-C-V cards in front of each team at the opposite end of the room. Tape a verse reference to the wall. On the "go" signal, the first player on each team will hop to the B-C-V cards and place the B card under the book title before hopping back to the line. The next players will hop to place the C (for "chapter") cards in place and so on. The first team to correctly position the B-C-V cards scores a point. Play until a team reaches five points. Then locate and read aloud the verse references.

For the word of the Lord is right and true. —Psalm 33:4

Looking for more great resources? You've come to the right place!

Object Talks

PRODUCT #	PRODUCT TITLE	PRICE PER ITEM	QUANTITY	TOTAL
1154-2	101 Simple Service Projects	$13.99		
1370-7	Quick Quiz Talk Starters	$13.99		
2022-4	Show Me! Devotions	$12.99		
7440-7	Show Me More! Object Talks	$12.99		
7441-7	20/20 Crafts & Object Talks	$10.99		
1417-7	Collect-n-Do Object Talks	$13.99		
1237-9	A to Z Object Talks (New Testament)	$5.99		
1236-0	A to Z Object Talks (Old Testament)	$5.99		
1838-X	Bible Message Make-n-Takes	$12.99		
1429-0	Preschool Bible Message Make-n-Takes	$12.99		
1184-4	Edible Object Talks (Jesus)	$5.99		
1183-6	Edible Object Talks (Values)	$5.99		

Crafts & Games

PRODUCT #	PRODUCT TITLE	PRICE PER ITEM	QUANTITY	TOTAL
7449-7	Larger-Than-Life Crafts & Service Projects	$10.99		
7441-7	20/20 Crafts & Object Talks	$10.99		
5695-7	Instant Games for Children's Ministry	$13.99		
1199-2	Collect-n-Play Games	$13.99		
1198-4	Collect-n-Make Crafts	$13.99		
1838-X	Bible Message Make-n-Takes	$12.99		

Bibles & Bible Storytelling

PRODUCT #	PRODUCT TITLE	PRICE PER ITEM	QUANTITY	TOTAL
7450-7	Kids-Tell-Em Bible Stories	$11.99		
0406-6	My Good Night Bible	$14.99		
1228-X	My Little Good Night Bible	$9.99		
1174-7	My Good Night Story Book	$14.99		
1229-8	My Little Good Night Story Book	$9.99		
1365-0	My Good Night Prayers	$14.99		
1522-X	Christmas With Night Light	$10.99		
1362-0	Bedtime for Night Light (coloring book)	$3.99		
1418-5	Collect-n-Tell Bible Stories	$13.99		

POWER BUILDERS (2-Year Curriculum)

PRODUCT #	PRODUCT TITLE	PRICE PER ITEM	QUANTITY	TOTAL
7550-7	Disciple Makers	$12.99		
7554-7	Faith Finders	$12.99		
7552-7	Servant Leaders	$12.99		
7556-7	Value Seekers	$12.99		
7551-7	Hope Finders	$12.99		
7555-7	Joy Builders	$12.99		
7557-7	Power Boosters	$12.99		
7553-7	Peace Makers	$12.99		

Teacher Ideas & Learning Centers

PRODUCT #	PRODUCT TITLE	PRICE PER ITEM	QUANTITY	TOTAL
5525-X	Saving Your Sanity (preschool)	$12.99		
7444-7	Instant Learning Fun-Folders OT (CD)	$9.99		
7445-7	Instant Learning Fun-Folders NT (CD)	$9.99		
1332-4	200+ Activities for Children's Ministry	$12.99		
7442-7	On & Off the Wall (Visual Teaching Tools)	$13.99		
7443-7	Classroom Celebrations!	$12.99		

Bible Memory, Bible Skills, & Worship Activities

PRODUCT #	PRODUCT TITLE	PRICE PER ITEM	QUANTITY	TOTAL
7446-7	Scripture Memory Makers	$12.99		
7445-7	Making Scripture Memorable	$12.99		
7448-7	Bible Skill Builders	$13.99		
7447-7	Worship Wow!	$12.99		

Best Buy!

You can order two easy ways:

1. Directly from *Susan Lingo Books* through check or money order, or

2. from Amazon.com.

Send your check or money order (including shipping and handling) along with your order to:

Susan Lingo Books
3310 N. Logan Ave.
Loveland, CO 80538

Handling ($1.50 per order)	$1.50
Shipping: **Standard Book Rate:** 1-3 books—$6.00 4+ books—$6.00 + $1.50 each additional book **Priority USPS:** 1 book—$7.00 2+ books—$7.00 + $4.00 each additional book	
Subtotal of S/H	
Subtotal of books ordered	
TOTAL ENCLOSED	

www.susanlingobooks.com

www.ingramcontent.com/pod-product-compliance
Lightning Source LLC
LaVergne TN
LVHW061314060426
835507LV00019B/2145